> Todd,
> January 22, 2023
> Ephesians 5:15,16
> Be encouraged to continue to make "the most of every opportunity" for the Hope community

SO WHAT WISDOM

Living Wisely With Eternity in View

Richard Van Yperen

RICHARD VAN YPEREN

WestBow Press
A DIVISION OF THOMAS NELSON
& ZONDERVAN

Copyright © 2022 Richard Van Yperen.

All rights reserved. No part of this book may be used or reproduced by any means, graphic, electronic, or mechanical, including photocopying, recording, taping or by any information storage retrieval system without the written permission of the author except in the case of brief quotations embodied in critical articles and reviews.

This book is a work of non-fiction. Unless otherwise noted, the author and the publisher make no explicit guarantees as to the accuracy of the information contained in this book and in some cases, names of people and places have been altered to protect their privacy.

WestBow Press books may be ordered through booksellers or by contacting:

WestBow Press
A Division of Thomas Nelson & Zondervan
1663 Liberty Drive
Bloomington, IN 47403
www.westbowpress.com
844-714-3454

Because of the dynamic nature of the Internet, any web addresses or links contained in this book may have changed since publication and may no longer be valid. The views expressed in this work are solely those of the author and do not necessarily reflect the views of the publisher, and the publisher hereby disclaims any responsibility for them.

Any people depicted in stock imagery provided by Getty Images are models, and such images are being used for illustrative purposes only.
Certain stock imagery © Getty Images.

Scripture quotations taken from The Holy Bible, New International Version® NIV® Copyright © 1973 1978 1984 2011 by Biblica, Inc. TM Used by permission. All rights reserved worldwide.

Scripture quotations marked (ESV) are from The ESV® Bible (The Holy Bible, English Standard Version®), copyright © 2001 by Crossway, a publishing ministry of Good News Publishers. Used by permission. All rights reserved.

ISBN: 978-1-6642-7130-2 (sc)
ISBN: 978-1-6642-7132-6 (hc)
ISBN: 978-1-6642-7131-9 (e)

Library of Congress Control Number: 2022912230

Print information available on the last page.

WestBow Press rev. date: 8/24/2022

CONTENTS

Testimonials vii
Acknowledgments ix
Preface xi
Introduction xvii

PART I: *Godly Wisdom Is Gospel Wisdom*

Chapter 1   From "at the Very Beginning" to "in the Beginning" 1
Chapter 2   The Power of Identity 10
Chapter 3   Sign Language 22
Chapter 4   On the Pathway to Belief 32
Chapter 5   A Samaritan Woman's Belief 44
Chapter 6   A Royal Official Believes 53
Chapter 7   Godly Wisdom Is Gospel Wisdom 58

PART II: *James's Godly Wisdom Instructions for Living Out the Gospel in a Post-Resurrection World*

Chapter 8   Single-Minded Faith 64
Chapter 9   True Listening 73
Chapter 10   Wisdom Rejects Favoritism 86
Chapter 11   Faith and Actions 92
Chapter 12   Now Listen 105
Chapter 13   Prayer Changes Lives 116
Chapter 14   So What? 126

TESTIMONIALS

As we navigate a world in which truth is thought to be relative, or even nonexistent, it is imperative that the pathway to Wisdom and Truth be either discovered for the first time or found again by those who may have lost their way through unrelenting false narratives of our time. Richard Van Yperen in his book *So What Wisdom* directs the reader back to Wisdom and Truth from above. The Bible's narrative is centered on God's one redemptive story and His unified plan for living in light of God's love for humankind. Van Yperen systematically presents wisdom as outlined by Solomon in Proverbs, the life and teaching of Jesus in the Gospels, and James's exhortations to the brethren in the book of James. His book systematically compares these teachings and, in so doing, uncovers their unity. Within *So What Wisdom*, readers will also examine the consequences of choosing worldly wisdom, grounded in man's self-centered thought (foolishness), as opposed to Wisdom as revealed by God. At a time of "false news" and a lack of trust abounds, readers will be refreshed by the knowledge that times may change but Wisdom, as recorded in God's Word, is unchangeable. Readers will be rewarded with insight that is more precious than thousands of pieces of silver and gold and the pleasant words that are like a honeycomb, sweet to the soul and healing to the bones (Prov. 16:24, Ps. 119:72).

Milton Uecker
Professor Emeritus, Columbia International University
Author and general editor of the Distinctively Christian series on a Christ-centered approach to early childhood and elementary education and ministry

I love how Richard practically points Solomon's wisdom to Jesus. He alone is the God of all wisdom. I'd encourage you to read this book and grow in the wisdom that Jesus gives to all who are ready to receive.

Jon Adams
Lead pastor, the Vine Community Church, Cumming, Georgia

Richard Van Yperen has been studying, teaching, and living the contents of this book for the past twenty years. His ability to ponder "so what" wisdom results in a deep dive into scripture and the meaning of life. By reading this book, you will be better equipped on earth to block out the noise and be transformed with an eternal perspective. Bottom line: Life will never be the same.

Darren Petersen
School district leader in NJ and adjunct professor at St. Peter's University

ACKNOWLEDGMENTS

I am grateful for the many insights I gained from men who studied scripture with me early weekday mornings, Saturday mornings, and weekday evenings over the past twenty-two years building a long line of Wise Guys.

A special thanks to Pastor Jon Adams, Kevin Neel, Andrew Culp, Darren Petersen, Ashley Smith, and Milton Uecker for their willingness to read my manuscript and offer feedback.

Finally, I am forever thankful for my wife, adult children, and grandchildren, who have patiently provided real-life ongoing opportunities for testing, applying, and learning *So What Wisdom*.

PREFACE

My physical life began in the midst of a blizzard on December 21, 1948, and my spiritual life began one unremarkable Sunday in 1959 when, as I sat listening to a sermon in Grace Church, I felt a stirring to accept Jesus as my Savior. However, in hindsight, that decision was more about declaring my alignment with a group of people and their rules for living than about being transformed by God's grace. For the majority of my life, I have struggled inwardly with inadequacy, deception, guilt, and shame. Essentially, I strove to appear outwardly perfect, while knowing deep down that my heart was desperately corrupt. But something occurred in my mid-forties. I was confronted with my past in such a way that I was forced to my knees in broken-hearted confession, recognizing my need for grace and mercy. For the first time, I recognized the truth in Proverbs 28:13. "He who conceals his sins does not prosper, but whoever confesses and renounces them finds mercy." When I deserved to be judged and rejected, God, through Jesus' death as the sacrifice we needed to cover our sins and resurrection, granted me uplifting joy and peace instead of crushing condemnation!

Until that transformative event of my life, I had no interest in godly wisdom. My all-consuming interest focused on maintaining an image, I found fulfillment in outward acts designed to influence admiration. Then I found myself, on my knees, recognizing my absolute need for a Savior, no longer able to deny the horror of my sins and the hurt they caused others. In that state of mind, as I meditated on my absolute need for God's grace and mercy, I hungered for knowledge and understanding of God and His purpose for me.

Vocationally, I was an educator working as a high school English teacher and coach. In those roles, I knew, instinctively, I had the gift of teaching. It was an undeniable gift from God. Supernaturally, I knew how to motivate students to learn. Before my transformation, I took that gift for granted. Now humbled, I saw that God's gift needed to be committed for God's purposes. That decision led me to leave public school teaching for a position at Rift Valley Academy, a school for missionary children in Kenya, East Africa. Those four years in a Christian school prepared me for the opportunity to become an administrator at Eastern Christian School in New Jersey for the next fifteen years, first as a principal and then as director of curriculum and instruction. In both roles, God equipped me to help others be effective and influential Christian educators of students from pre-K through twelfth grade.

During this time, as director of curriculum and instruction for a private Christian school, Solomon's wisdom book of Proverbs piqued my interest, and I found myself leading a men's study group based on Proverbs 1–9. As we studied these nine chapters, it became clear to me that the content was actually a well-designed curriculum for parents to use to teach their children about godly wisdom. That first group over twenty years ago labeled themselves Wise Guys. Since then, I have been leading men's groups in a study of Solomon's God-given curriculum. Those studies led to my first book, *A Complete Guide to Godly Wisdom: 17 Wisdom Precepts from the Perfect Father Based on Proverbs 1–9*. Over time, our Wise Guys' study expanded to include the first four chapters of the Gospel of John, and James's letter to believers, which has led to this book. *So What Wisdom* is intended to show how the apostles John and James reveal what it looks like to live out godly wisdom. More than ever, our world desperately needs the Good News that we can experience abundant life, now and forevermore.

One more explanation: All curricula must minimally answer two questions: *what* and *why*. Curriculum that genuinely influences learning must describe what is to be learned and why it must be learned. However, knowing what needs to be learned and why it needs to be learned only prepares a pathway to learning. I have found there is one other question that is absolutely necessary for lasting learning: the question is *so what?*

The *what* and *why* explanations are like GPS directions to an on-ramp toward learning. When a teacher provides structured lessons that open up opportunities to *apply* learning, the learning becomes understanding, and understanding leads to learning that is transformational.

Great athletic coaches know how to lead athletes to successfully apply head knowledge that validates a desired goal. Great coaches spend minimal time lecturing about techniques, theories, and rules—the *what*s of a sport that every athlete needs to know. Effective coaches understand their athletes need to apply what they have heard by practicing the sport to fully comprehend *why* they need to know the *what*s. But just knowing about that need does not make one proficient. No coach worth her/his salt would then say, "My job is done," when the athlete can demonstrate head knowledge about the sport. Head knowledge qualifies the athlete to be a commentator, not a competitor. It is in their repetitive experiences at practicing that athletes begin to desire to become proficient. That desired effect is the beginning of an answer to the "So what?" question, and this is where the coach can make the greatest difference—by breaking down skills needed, giving drills to teach those skills, and then combining each individual skill into proficient performance. It is in the discipline of practice that an athlete begins to figure out the answer to the "So what?" question. Great coaches are educators who provide experiences and environments for their pupils to put into action what they have learned. Any athlete will testify that the way to proficiency is in the struggle to translate head knowledge into expertise. However, expertise is only confirmed and validated in competition. Competitors discover the answer to the "So what?" question by doing and applying all they learned. Performance is the completive action that addresses the "So what?" of learning.

During the 2021 World Series between the Atlanta Braves and the Houston Astros, a commentator told a story about Freddie Freeman, the Braves' first baseman, who had won the National League batting title in 2020 and had led his team in home runs in 2021. The commentator recalled that Freddie was such a naturally gifted hitter even in T-ball that the coaches moved him up to playing with boys much older than Freddie. *Wikipedia* recalls the same assertion: "At the age of six, Freeman practiced with Little_

League ball players, who were twice his age. Aged seven, he was placed on a team of nine-year-olds. When Freeman himself turned nine, he was assigned to play with the team of twelve-year-olds."

His natural ability made him so successful in high school that he signed a minor league contract after high school. However, despite his giftedness, Freddie struck out every time he came to bat. He knew what he wanted to do and he knew why he wanted to do it, but for the first time as a baseball player knowing was not enough. So out of frustration, he called his dad, telling him that he was going to quit. Having watched his son try so hard, his dad told him that he was striking out because he was swinging at every pitch. He recommended that Freddie not swing at any pitches when he came to the plate. Taking his father's advice, Freddie came to bat, refused to swing, and he walked on four pitches. So Freddie continued to refuse to swing and continued to walk. Finally, opposing pitchers knew that Freddie would not swing so they started pitching strikes, and in the next at bat Freddie got his first hit in the minors—a homerun! As a young phenom, Freddie naturally knew *what* he needed to do—swing his bat. For him there was no need for learning the fundamentals of batting until he experienced failure and frustration. The beginning of success in professional baseball came when he was forced to ask the question: *So what* do I need to do to succeed at the highest level of his profession? He learned patience and discipline that allowed him to use his eye-and-hand coordination to hit a 90mph fastball and the myriad pitches professional pitchers use to strike out hitters.

Dr. Stan Beecham, a sports psychologist and leadership consultant, writes in his book, *Elite Minds: How Winners Think Differently to Create a Competitive Edge and Maximize Success* (McGraw-Hill Education, 2017), describes how the concept of practice in sports expects that "one will make mistakes while trying to develop a skill." On the other hand,

> Business has not yet incorporated the concept of practice into its milieu. Every meeting and conversation is a game, not practice. Every day is a game day. This makes mistakes much more costly, and it also increases the chance that

the same mistake will be repeated ... Both corporate and educational systems are very didactic, focusing on reading and listening instead of experimenting and doing. Success is defined by memorizing the right answer ... That system is not effective in bringing about changes of behavior. (p. 32)

Beecham's "concept of practice" is what needs to happen in all learning. For example, academic learning too often settles for learning objectives that produce memorized regurgitation of knowledge, forgetting that *completed* learning demands guided practice for performance that demonstrates proficiency. When a learner is challenged and motivated to answer the "So what?" question through trial and error, authentic learning becomes anchored and lasting. In other words, a person only becomes a true learner when he/she applies the learning through performance. Great teachers create challenging practice projects that force students to apply rather than regurgitate what they are learning.

This book is entitled *So What Wisdom* because it answers the "So what?" questions about godly wisdom for you, and for me. No doubt Solomon's extraordinary curriculum in Proverbs 1–9 provides head knowledge that motivated sons and daughters to learn and follow wisdom precepts designed to avoid living foolishly while enabling flourishing, but it didn't answer the ultimate "So what?" question: "My ultimate end is death, *so what* is the point?" Yes, Proverbs provides compelling answers to the questions "*What* is godly wisdom?" and "*Why* should one get it?" But at the end of one's life, the answers to the "So what?" question addresses only the past, not eternity. Proverbs 1–9 teaches about how godly wisdom allows one to thrive in a sinful world. However, Solomon's teaching provided an incomplete answer to the "So what?" question because the embodiment of godly wisdom, Jesus Christ, had not yet entered the world.

Old Testament wisdom established a pathway that would eventually lead to a destination through the redemptive death and resurrection of the one who is "the way, the truth and the life" (John 14:6) for all who believe in Jesus Christ. Without Jesus Christ as the embodiment of eternal godly wisdom, we are likely to slip into trying to apply the wisdom of Solomon to perform our way through life like the Pharisees, who were masters of religious performance but alienated from God.

My premise in this book is that Solomon's teaching about the beginning of wisdom in Proverbs 1–9 is completed in the person of Jesus Christ, as shown in the first four chapters of John's Gospel and applied in James's letter "to the twelve tribes scattered among the nations" (James 1:1). In part I, we will look at the "what," "why," and "so what" answers that Jesus modeled, taught, and promised about godly wisdom in John's first four chapters of his gospel. Finally, having established Jesus' teaching of the What and the Why in part 1, we will look at James's eight "so what" practices for developing the disposition of living out mature post-resurrection wisdom with eternity in view in part 2.

INTRODUCTION

> A shoot will come up from the stump of Jesse, and from his roots a Branch will bear fruit. The Spirit of the LORD will rest on him—the Spirit of wisdom and of understanding, the Spirit of counsel and of power, the Spirit of knowledge and of the fear of the LORD—and he will delight in the fear of the LORD.
> — Isaiah 11:1–3

IN THE BEGINNING

All created matter has a moment in time we call a beginning. For example, this book has a beginning, page 1, and because it has a beginning, it follows that it will have an ending page. On the other hand, it could be argued that this book will have a continued existence after the last physical ending page. if this is archived, it may have a longer life. Nevertheless, the law of creation states that if it has a beginning, it has a life span that necessitates an eventual ending. Having an ending is the essence of being temporal. The quality of being temporal is one of the primary meanings of the term "worldly" when we describe all that exists in the created world.

As entities in the created world, you and I have physical bodies that have a beginning in time and a life span within time. I am aware my body is temporary because I experience the aging process that presages my demise. Yet there is something within me that yearns for the eternal. That something, my soul, causes me to search and explore our wonderful world for permanence while finding only temporariness everywhere.

Because eternity cannot be found in our temporary physical body or in our possessions, we are driven to seek our soul's eternal design.

The Bible describes the beginning of the created world in Genesis. This book of beginnings begins with, "In the beginning God created the heavens and the earth" (Gen. 1:1) God's six days of creation mark a beginning of time that implies that before this action, there was no beginning because nothing was created. God had no beginning and therefore has no ending. Nothing temporal existed before God created the world.

God created humankind as His crowning work. "Then God said, 'Let us make man in our image, in our likeness, and let them rule'" (Gen. 1:26). Adam and Eve had God's favor to rule over all that was created. "God saw all that he had made, and it was very good" (Gen. 1:21). In the beginning, Adam and Eve were created with the ability to choose good or evil, bearing the image of the eternal Creator God.

> Now the LORD God had planted a garden in the east, in Eden; and there he put man he had formed. And the LORD God made all kinds of trees grow out of the ground—trees that were pleasing to the eye and good for food ... The LORD God took the man and put him in the Garden of Eden to work it and take care of it. And the LORD God commanded the man, "You are free to eat from any tree in the garden; but you must not eat from the tree of knowledge of good and evil, for when you eat of it you will surely die." (Gen. 2:8, 2:9, 2:15–17)

Adam and Eve had trees and plants that were good for food and pleasing to the eye, and they had an abiding harmonious relationship with the Source of all knowledge and wisdom. But when they were tempted to disobey their Creator, they chose *worldly* wisdom even though they had unlimited access to *godly* wisdom. This is called the original sin. Their choice of satisfying their temporal desires in the beginning set a pattern that all humankind has had to wrestle with—the temptation of choosing temporal sensual gratifications of the world rather than choosing to delay gratification for the benefits of eternal values. The power of gratifying temporal sensuality is the essence of worldly wisdom in a world full of unfulfilled desires that promise much but deliver disappointment and death. Adam and Eve and their early family members lived extraordinarily long lives, but they eventually died, and as their ancestors multiplied, brokenness grew as life spans steadily declined.

Then in the tenth century BC, Solomon, the author and compiler of the book of Proverbs, created a much-needed curriculum for teaching young people how to thrive in a sinful and broken world by gaining godly wisdom for making wise life-giving decisions. Interestingly, his curriculum, designed for parental instruction of children, uses the word "beginning" in its statements of its primary theme in Proverbs 1:7 and 9:10.

> The fear of the LORD is the *beginning* of knowledge, but fools despise wisdom and discipline. (Prov. 1:7)
>
> The fear of the LORD is the *beginning* of wisdom, and knowledge of the Holy One is understanding. (Prov. 9:10)

Adam and Eve foolishly rejected their reverential fear of the LORD in favor of their desire to be equal to God. In other words, by choosing worldly wisdom, Adam and Eve sentenced themselves to painful temporariness that dominated and damaged that essential part in them that yearned for everlastingness—their soul—and separated them from a relationship with God. Solomon, arguably the wisest, yet most worldly, man who ever lived, recognized the need to teach that all godly wisdom begins with a fearful reverence for our eternal Creator. In the first nine chapters of Proverbs, Solomon offers a complete guide for godly wisdom. While his instructive precepts served as a map for a pathway to finding godly wisdom in one's life journey in a temporal world, they lacked the power to overcome the inevitable final destination of every earthly life journey—death. His wisdom precepts could only point to a future fulfillment of godly wisdom embodied in a Savior who would break our bonds of sin's curse. By perfectly living out godly wisdom while still taking on the curse for our sins, Jesus provided a way to have what our soul longs for—forgiveness for our sins and eternal life.

Over four hundred years after Solomon recorded Proverbs, the apostle John, in the first century AD, opens his Gospel using the word "genesis" from the Greek word *gneseou*, translated "beginning."

> In the *beginning* was the Word, and the Word was with God and the Word was God. He was with God in the *beginning*. (John 1:1, 2)

John introduces Jesus Christ, who was present at the creation of the world, declaring

> Through him all things were made; without him nothing was made that has been made. In him was life, and that life was the light of men. (John 1:3, 4)

John describes Jesus as the Word—the eternal One who brought meaning to all that was created at the beginning. He existed with God, and through Him all created things were made. He existed outside time before the beginning, having no beginning, and therefore no ending. In John's Gospel, he asserts that Jesus was born into the temporal world as a human to embody completive godly wisdom that lights the way to eternal life for whoever believes in Him.

Before Jesus' life, death, and resurrection, humankind had the law of Moses and Solomon's curriculum as guides to right living and godly wisdom. However, John writes, "Grace and truth came through Jesus Christ. No one has ever seen God, but God the One and Only, who is at the Father's side, has made him known" (John 1:17, 18). John's Gospel was written to share the good news that in Jesus' life, death, and resurrection, Jesus modeled the eternal values of godly wisdom, declaring that He is "the way, and the truth, and the life" (John 14:9). Before the arrival of Jesus, Moses had delivered the laws for holy living, and Solomon had taught the precepts for living wisely. The Old Testament laws and precepts for godly wisdom provided a complete guide to knowledge and understanding for holy and wise living in a world corrupted by sin. On the other hand, Jesus modeled and perfectly fulfilled the law while embodying godly wisdom, so that through believing in Him and His sacrifice that is a substitute for our sins, we can receive the Spirit of wisdom and eternal favor through His grace.

Furthermore, James, the brother of Jesus, completes what Solomon had instructed and Jesus had modeled by clarifying eight exhortations for what godly wisdom–living looks like for believers in a post-resurrection world. Solomon's seventeen "My son" instructions provide the template for James's eight "My brothers" directions. Taken all together, James's eight instructions form a practical completive guide for believers to live out eternal kingdom values. However, the intent is not to just influence believers to be wiser. In his concluding sentence of his letter to his brother believers, he writes, "Remember this: Whoever turns a sinner from the error of his way will save him from death and cover a multitude of sins" (James 5:20). James is writing to believers to remind them of their responsibility to complete Jesus' mission to seek and save the lost.

SO WHAT?

The purpose of this book is to explore answers to the all-important "So what?" questions that complete Solomon's curriculum (Prov. 1–9) about godly wisdom, through John's Gospel of Jesus Christ and James's instructions for living out godly wisdom in a post-resurrection world. In the first four chapters of his gospel of Jesus Christ, John describes how Jesus demonstrates the importance of belief in discerning truth as he reveals that He is the way, the truth, and the life. James's letter challenges believers to demonstrate specific actions of godly wisdom in our current post-resurrection circumstances so that many will be turned from the error of their ways.

INTRODUCTION STUDY GUIDE

Review Proverbs 8:1–36.

- List the repeated wisdom vocabulary in Proverbs 8:1–14. (Examples in italics for first bullet.)
  - Proverbs 8:1, 5
    Understanding
    Prudence

  - Proverbs 8:5, 12

  - Proverbs 8:6

  - Proverbs 8:9

  - Proverbs 8:10

  - Proverbs 8:9, 10, 12

  - Proverbs 8:12

  - Proverbs 8:14

- Wisdom declares her characteristics in Proverbs 8:15–31. Finish each statement below:
  - By me ... _____
  - I love ... _____
  - With me ... _____
  - I walk ... _____
  - The LORD brought me forth as ... _____
  - I was appointed ... _____
  - I was there when ... _____
  _____
  _____
  _____
  - Then I was ... _____
- Wisdom promises in Proverbs 8:32–36. Finish the following statements:
  - Blessed are those who ...

  - Blessed is the man who ...

  - Whoever finds me finds ...

  - All who hate me ...

Fill in the blanks in the following quotes:

"From the beginning" (Prov. 8:3) to "In the beginning" (John 1:1)

- Jesus was _____ _____ "in the beginning," and through Him all things were _____."
- "To those whom God has called ... Christ the power of God and the _____ of God." (1 Corinthians 1:20-24)

Solomon concludes his Wisdom curriculum, restating his theme:

> The fear of the LORD is the *beginning* of _____, and knowledge of the Holy One is understanding. (Prov. 9:10)

John begins his gospel declaring that the Holy One is the Word who was with God in the beginning of all creation and

> The Word became flesh and made His dwelling among us ... the One and Only who came from the Father, full of _____ and _____. (John 1:14)

James concludes his epistle to Christ followers scattered among the nations in the first century challenging them with the mission to

> remember this: Whoever turns a sinner from the error of his way will _____ _____ from death and cover a multitude of sins. (James 5:20)

This 40,000 feet view of the Bible's scope of godly wisdom is summarized in Hebrews 1:1, 2:

> In the past God spoke to our forefathers through the prophets at many times and in various ways, but in these last days He has spoken to us by His Son, whom he appointed heir of ___ _____, and through whom He made ___ _____.

So what connections do you see that help you understand godly wisdom in the verses above?

PART I

GODLY WISDOM IS GOSPEL WISDOM

FROM "AT THE VERY BEGINNING" TO "IN THE BEGINNING"

(John 1:1–18)

Worldly wisdom is natural. Godly wisdom is unnatural. While both worldly wisdom and godly wisdom are rooted in human desires for gratification, the first craves immediate gratification and the second knows the value of delayed gratification satisfied in God alone. Our sensual bodies' and hearts' desires naturally conspire to get satisfaction immediately. We don't need to learn this. From birth, we cry out, essentially demanding, "My will, not thy will." Godly wisdom, on the other hand, must be taught, modeled, and learned often through trial and error. The attainment of godly wisdom requires intentionality and determination to "call out for insight and cry aloud for understanding, and look for it as for silver and search for it as for hidden treasure" (Prov. 2:3–4).

To demonstrate contrasting attributes between worldly wisdom and godly wisdom, Solomon personifies worldly wisdom as Lady Folly and godly wisdom as Lady Wisdom. Lady Folly, also called the Adulteress, embodies careless, sensuous gratification, while Lady Wisdom embodies prudent delaying of gratification in pursuit of understanding and knowledge. Both women advertise and appeal to those who are simple.

Lady Folly "is loud; she is undisciplined and without knowledge ... calling out to those who pass by ... 'Let all who are simple come in here! ... Stolen water is sweet; food eaten in secret is delicious!'" (Prov. 9:13–17).

Lady Wisdom "has built her house ... She has [prepared a formal banquet]. She has sent out her maids, and she calls from the highest point of the city. 'Let all who are simple come in here! ... Leave your simple ways and you will live; walk in the way of understanding'" (Prov. 9:1–4, 6).

Previously in Solomon's curriculum, he dedicated one chapter for each of his women to voice her mode of persuasion. Proverbs 7 provides a titillating anecdote that displays Lady Folly's seduction of a simple youth. Proverbs 8 displays Lady Wisdom's earnest argument for following godly wisdom's eternal values. By juxtaposing each woman's appeal to young novices, Solomon graphically portrays the sway of sensuality versus the reign of reason.

In Proverbs 8:22–31, Solomon has Lady Wisdom recite an autobiographical hymn, describing her role in creation as a rebuttal to the temporary, sensual gratification Lady Folly offers.

> The Lord brought me forth as the first of his works,
> before his deeds of old;
> I was formed long ages ago,
> At the very beginning, when the world came to be.
> When there were no watery depths, I was given birth,
> when there were no springs overflowing with water;
> before the mountains were settled in place,
> before the hills, I was given birth,
> before he made the world or its fields
> or any of the dust of the earth.
> I was there when he set the heavens in place,
> when he marked out the horizon on the face of the deep,
> when he established the clouds above
> and fixed securely the fountains of the deep,
> when he gave the sea its boundary

> so the waters would not overstep his command,
> and when he marked out the foundations of the earth.
> Then I was constantly at his side.
> I was filled with delight day after day,
> rejoicing always in his presence,
> rejoicing in his whole world
> and delighting in mankind.

Lady Wisdom's poetic description of her résumé points to an intimate relationship with the Almighty Creator of all things. These extraordinarily beautiful words in this hymn are a foreshadowing of the eternal truth of John's words over four hundred years later, which introduced the final Word: "In the beginning was the Word and the Word was with God, and the Word was God" (John 1:1). In both passages, wisdom is identified as a pre-creation attribute of God that existed before time and has no beginning or ending. Godly wisdom is an eternal attribute. This is a really big deal! Conversely, Lady Folly's worldly wisdom has it's beginning, and thus its eventual ending—the grave—like all things in the natural world because of the actions of Adam and Eve.

SOLOMON'S THEME BRIDGED BY JOHN'S THEME

In the last chapter of his wisdom curriculum, Solomon restates his theme: "The fear of the Lord is the beginning of wisdom, and knowledge of the Holy One is understanding." (Prov. 9:10). This theme, that wisdom is learned through reverence for the Lord while acknowledging that God is God and we are not, is foundational to godly wisdom. Reverence for the Lord demands that I must trust in Him "with all my heart and lean not on my own understanding," which is grounded in worldly reasoning (Prov. 3:5).

John writes his theme in John 1:10–13:

> He [Jesus] was in the world, and though the world was
> made through him, the world did not recognize him, He

came to that which was his own, but his own did not receive him. Yet to all who received him, to those who believed in his name, he gave the right to become children of God—children born not of natural descent, nor of human decision or a husband's will, but born of God.

John's theme addresses the "So what?" of Solomon's theme. Solomon could only describe the beginning of godly wisdom in anticipation of the Messiah's completive invitation to be born of God into His eternal kingdom. The eternal One, Jesus, who existed outside of time, enters into time to offer us, whom He created, eternal life as adopted children of God.

Now, over two thousand years later, we are privileged to live in the post-resurrection time when God is executing His plan of restoration of all creation. We have the awesome advantage of hindsight to see the completive biblical story of creation, fall, redemption, and now, the post-resurrection time of restoration before Christ's return. Yet our need for godly wisdom in our temporal world, full of distractions and sensuality appealing to all our senses, has never been greater. The ubiquitous cacophony of voices that call us to the pursuit and gratification of temporal worldly desires can drown out God's singular call for us to be born of God as heirs to His eternal kingdom. Figuratively, the descendants of Lady Folly or Lady Wisdom influencers are more active than ever thousands of years after Solomon's curriculum, John's Gospel, and James's letter.

Proverbs 1:1–7 and John 1:1–18 Theme Vocabulary

Solomon begins his treatise about godly wisdom by introducing key vocabulary that describes the essential elements of godly wisdom. (Take a moment and mentally try to define godly wisdom. What words would you use?) Solomon's vocabulary in the verses that introduce his theme verse in Proverbs 1:7 includes "understanding," "prudent," "prudence," "knowledge," "discretion," and "discerning." These words by themselves would describe all kinds of wisdom. However, the theme verse qualifies this list as essential aspects of divine transformative wisdom.

> The *fear* of the LORD is the beginning of knowledge, but fools despise wisdom and discipline. (Prov. 1:7, emphasis mine)

Fear—a profound, sober reverence—of the Creator Lord of all created things provides the lens through which we view understanding, prudence, knowledge, discretion, and discernment as essential attributes of godly wisdom. This vocabulary is repeated over and over in the ensuing wisdom curriculum in Proverbs 1–9. Solomon's theme implies that fools hate and reject the vocabulary of godly wisdom because fools despise submission and discipline while valuing all things temporal for immediate gain with no thought of eventual consequences.

Centuries after Solomon's book of Proverbs, the apostle John begins his gospel account with the vocabulary of figurative language. Jesus is called "the Word." He is described as the "light of men" (John 1:4) and "the light that shines in the darkness" (John 1:5). In fact, "light" is repeated eight times in the first nine verses. John the Baptist is introduced as a "witness to testify concerning that light" (John 1:7), declaring "the true light that gives light to every man was coming into the world" (John 1:9).

Conversely, "darkness" is mentioned twice and implied multiple times. The contrast between light and darkness is a constant motif throughout John's Gospel. Just as light provides sight and clarity in a dark room, Jesus is portrayed from the beginning of John's Gospel as the light that reveals and clarifies spiritual knowledge and understanding, which are the building blocks of godly wisdom in the midst of the darkness of worldly wisdom.

John's introduction of the Lord Jesus as the divine Word who brings light into darkness declares that Jesus is "light to every man" (John 1:9). That light provides understanding, knowledge, prudence, and the fruit of all goodness, righteousness, and truth. John is declaring that Jesus is the final Word of godly wisdom.

Later in Apostle Paul's New Testament epistle to the Ephesian church, Paul picks up on this theme:

> For you were once *darkness*, but now you are *light* in the Lord. Live as children of *light* (for the fruit of the *light* consists in all goodness, righteousness and truth) and find out what pleases the Lord. Have nothing to do with the fruitless deeds of *darkness*, but rather expose them. (Eph. 5:8–11)

In exhorting Ephesian believers to "find out what pleases the Lord" (Eph. 5:10), Paul echoes Solomon's exhortation to "fear the LORD" (Prov. 1:7), as well as John's motifs of darkness and light.

"Believe" is another important thematic word that is repeated in John 1:7 and 12 and will be repeated throughout the entire Gospel of John. John the author introduces John the Baptist as "a witness to testify concerning that light, so that through him [Jesus] all men might believe" (John 1:7). The overall theme of John's Gospel follows in John 1:12: "to all who received him [Jesus], to those who *believed* in his name he gave the right to become children of God—children born not of natural descent, nor of human decision or a husband's will, but born of God."

SO WHAT?

Solomon and John in their introductions describe godly wisdom by highlighting thematic words. But more to the point, both introductions present big ideas that are about the beginning of becoming reconciled with the Lord. Like Solomon's introduction to his godly wisdom curriculum that begins with a profound reverence for the LORD (Prov. 1:7), John, in his introduction to his gospel about Jesus, uses vocabulary designed to be the language that points to the beginning of believing in Jesus' offer of adoption into God's family: "To all who received [Jesus], to those who believed in his name, he gave the right to become children of God – children born not of natural descent, nor of human decision or a husband's will, but born of God" (John 1:12).

More than four hundred years after Solomon wrote his godly wisdom curriculum, John writes about "the Word [who] became flesh … who came from the Father, full of grace and truth" (John 1:14). Solomon's instruction about godly wisdom promised that "whoever finds me [wisdom] finds life and receives favor from the LORD" (Prov. 8:34). John identifies Jesus as the embodiment of godly wisdom, and whoever finds Him and believes in Him finds "the right to become children of God" (John 1:12b). Godly wisdom has a name—Jesus!

Jesus entered our world of life and death to offer us eternal life as children of God. The amazing gift of being adopted into the family of the Almighty Creator God is available to all who believe in Jesus. But what does it mean to believe in Jesus?

Grace and truth is the name of the first stop of our journey on the throughway of godly wisdom. We are invited to consider how grace and truth leads us to believe in the Word and receive "the right to become children of God" (John 1:12). How do you respond to that invitation?

So what do you think grace and truth have to do with wisdom?

CHAPTER 1 JOHN 1:1–18 STUDY GUIDE

1. Read John 20:31. At the end of his gospel account, John states his purpose. What is the keyword that is repeated in this verse?

2. Read John 1:14. At the beginning of his gospel, John introduces Jesus as the "One and Only who came from the Father, full of _____ and _____."
   a. Why do you think those two words are selected and repeated in John 1:16 and 17?

3. What makes John's Gospel unique?
   - Contrast the beginning of the other three gospels. How is John's introduction/beginning different from the other gospels?

   - John's Gospel begins with figurative language. Count the number of times each of the following words occur in this passage.
     - word _____
     - life _____
     - light _____
     - darkness _____
     - world _____
   - John 1:11–14
     - Summarize the big idea/theme

- Who are the main characters (John 1:1–18)?

- John 1:17, 18 Why is this good news?

APPLICATION

How does John's theme further your knowledge and understanding of God?

2

THE POWER OF IDENTITY

(John 1:19–51)

After his introduction and statement of the theme, John begins his narrative of Jesus' ministry, a story that in the future will be recognized as the Greatest Story Ever Told. The story begins when John the Baptist is approached by priests and Levites to question him about his identity. Apparently, this event occurred a day before he saw Jesus coming toward him, setting up a three "next day" narration that leads to a description of Jesus performing His first miraculous sign on the third day at a wedding in Cana in Galilee.

Clearly, this is not a "Once upon a time" story that follows a formulaic format ending with "happily ever after." This reads more like journalistic reporting on events leading to the most historic world-changing event of all time. John, the author, means to establish factual historical details through purposeful narration to support his big idea that Jesus is the long-awaited Messiah.

John begins by reporting on John the Baptist's interview with priests and Levites in a place "at Bethany on the other side of the Jordan, where John was baptizing" (John 1:28). He has attracted a crowd and a movement that has caught the attention of the Jewish elite. John's answer in response to their "Who are you?" question is a quote from Isaiah, "I am the voice of one calling in the desert, 'Make straight the way for the Lord'" (Isa.

40:3). His citation from Isaiah provokes some of the Pharisees to ask a loaded question: "Why then do you baptize if you are not the Christ, not Elijah, not the Prophet?" (John 1:25). The tone of their question implies a challenge to John's identity. His entire mission and ministry are being questioned by suggesting he is not qualified. As a man who has attracted hundreds of followers, John's humble response demonstrates a conviction driven by a clear sense of calling and identity.

> I baptize with water, but among you stands one you do not know. He is the one who comes after me, the thongs of whose sandals I am not worthy to untie. (John 1:26)

Popularity has not corrupted John's view of himself. Given the opportunity to proudly respond to their challenge, he humbly points away from himself to "the one who comes after" him.

At this point, it is worth remembering John the Baptist's story. Luke, in his gospel, reported that when Mary, pregnant with Jesus, visited Elizabeth, who was pregnant with John, he "leaped in her womb" (Luke 1:41). Even before Elizabeth was pregnant, an angel of the Lord appeared to Zechariah announcing that Elizabeth will give birth to a child who "will be a joy and delight ... and many will rejoice ... for he will be great in the sight of the Lord" (Luke 1:13a–15). Furthermore, Gabriel told Zechariah, "Many of the people of Israel he will bring back to the Lord their God. And he will go on before the Lord, in the spirit and power of Elijah, to turn the hearts of fathers to their children and the disobedient to the wisdom of righteousness—to make ready a people prepared for the Lord" (Luke 1:16, 17). Imagine being told by your parents that the angel Gabriel predicted greatness for you. What would that do for your perspective on your role and purpose?

The religious elite who were challenging John would recognize immediately that John is claiming to be the fulfillment of Isaiah's redemptive prophecy as well as Malachi's day of judgment prophecy in Malachi 2:17–3:1. And while John (the author) does not report on the full conversation between John (the Baptist) and the religious elite, Matthew does:

> But when he [John] saw many of the Pharisees and Sadducees coming to where he was baptizing, he said to them: "You brood of vipers! Who warned you to flee from the coming wrath? Produce fruit in keeping with repentance ... The ax is already at the root of the trees, and every tree that does not produce good fruit will be cut down and thrown into the fire." (Matt. 3:7–8, 3:10)

This is not a warm greeting! However, John's sense of identity emboldened him to stand firm in his calling and purpose in the face of contention and challenge. From before his birth, he had a clear calling. Undoubtedly, Zechariah and Elizabeth anchored that calling by telling him the remarkable story of an impossible pregnancy foretold by the angel of the Lord. John did not spontaneously decide to be a baptizer on a whim. His parents played an essential role in guiding and instructing him so that he recognized and responded when he was called to prepare the way for the Lord.

SO WHAT?

Zechariah and Elizabeth are real-life New Testament examples of Solomon's fictional father and mother instructors in Proverbs 1–9 who intentionally provide seventeen "my son" precepts for learning to choose to be wise rather than foolish. As wise, godly parents, they knew calling precedes identity, and they needed to pave the pathway to identity by teaching their child that he is made in the image of God for a God-given unique purpose.

You may say, "OK, but I know my parents never had a visit from Gabriel." On the other hand, our parents had God's Word and inspired words—four gospels, Acts, Paul's letters, Peter's letters, James's instructions, etc. Although it would be easy to blame our parents, we are without excuse too, because we also have God's word and wisdom in so many forms—podcasts, sermons, commentaries, and revealed truth—to help us discern our calling and identity.

So what is your calling? Do you believe you were created by God for a purpose? If so, what is that purpose? The answers to these questions establish your identity. Your answers will reveal whether you acknowledge that your identity comes from God. We are free to establish an identity that appeals to us, but like Solomon's pathway metaphor in Proverbs, our choice will lead to either life or destruction. Choosing to discern God's calling puts us on the pathway of life because we are wisely following God's design for our life. However, choosing to select your own identity, your own purpose, and your own pathway is an act of individualistic autonomy that eventually leads to brokenness because it rejects the design of your Creator.

WISDOM INSIGHT

What is the difference between ambition and calling? Basically, ambition originates within your desires and dreams for your future while a true calling, like John the Baptist's, is missional, pointing away from ambition and toward God's purpose and glory. What is your story about your calling? The apostle Paul, who has his own remarkable story of his calling on the road to Damascus when he heard a voice calling him away from his ambition to persecute Christians, writes in his well-known Romans 8 passage "that in all things God works for the good of those who love him, who have been *called* according to his purpose" (Rom. 8:28, my emphasis)

"THE NEXT DAY" #1 (JOHN 1:29–34)

Back to the author's narration: Like all good narrators, John draws his readers into his story with sequential words that create a timeline. Look at John 1:19, 29, 35, and 43 in chapter 1. John's first word of his narrative, "now," establishes a moment from which all that happens can be sequenced. Then for each subsequent narrative event in chapter 1, he starts with "The next day."

On the first "next day," John the Baptist sees Jesus approaching and immediately recognizes Him as "the Lamb of God, who takes away the sin of the world" (John 1:29). John, true to his calling, humbly declares Jesus as the one who replaces him and testifies that Jesus is "the Son of God."

> Each next "next day" narration repeats variations of two little words—*saw* and *said*. For example, in this first-day narration:
> (John 1:29) "John *saw* Jesus coming toward him and *said* …"
> (John 1:32) "Then John gave this *testimony* [*saying*]: 'I *saw* the Spirit come down from heaven as a dove and remain on him.'"
> (John 1:33) "I would not have known him, except the one who sent me to baptize with water *told* me, 'the man on whom you *see* the Spirit come down and remain is he who will baptize with the Holy Spirit.'"
> (John 1:34) "I have *seen* and I *testify* that this is the Son of God."

These little words and their synonyms emphasize the facts declared by a witness who saw and said what he saw. But there is an even more important emphasis that will grow stronger in John's narration of the events over the three next days.

"THE NEXT DAY" #2 (JOHN 1: 35–42)

On day 2, John the Baptizer is with two of his disciples when he *saw* Jesus passing by and "he *said*, 'Look the Lamb of God!'" (John 1:35) Two of his disciples heard him, and they left John to follow Jesus. This event leads to John the author's recording of Jesus' first words in the narration. Jesus turns toward the two disciples and *asks* them "What do you want?" (John 1:38) John records the conversation that follows:

> They *said*, "Rabbi" (which means Teacher), "where are you staying?"

"Come," he replied, "and you will *see*." (John 1:38, 39)

This is the first of two recorded conversations John chooses for his narration. Of all the words likely spoken on this day, why does John record these conversations? Look at the second conversation as recorded by John in John 1:40–42. One of the men who had gone with Jesus and *saw* where He was staying immediately turned around to find his brother to *tell* him, "We have found the Messiah." When he brought his brother to Jesus, "Jesus *looked* at him and *said*, 'You are Simon, son of John, you will be called Cephas'" (John 1:42).

John's reporting on the first day begins with one witness and testifier and expands to three witnesses who testify that Jesus is the Messiah on the second day, and on the second day, Jesus' first words to His first disciples are future oriented:

> Come … and you will see. (John 1:39)
> You are Simon son of John. You will be called Cephas. [Peter] (John 1:42)

"THE NEXT DAY" #3 (JOHN 1:43–51)

Then on the third next day, two more disciples are introduced. Jesus approaches Phillip and invites him to follow Him. Phillip finds Nathanael and *tells* him about Jesus. Nathanael is skeptical. So Phillip invites him to "come and *see*" (John 1:46).

This invitation leads to an important conversation between Jesus and Nathanael about what it means to believe. Jesus *sees* Nathanael approaching, and He describes Nathanael's character. Of course, in his skepticism, Nathanael *asks*, "How do you know me?" When Jesus *tells* him that He *saw* him under a fig tree without having been there, Nathanael immediately *declares* Jesus as "the Son of God; you are the King of Israel" (John 1:49).

SO WHAT?

On the first day, John the Baptist identifies that Jesus is "the Lamb of God." On the second day, in addition to John, Andrew declares that he has found the Messiah. And now on the third day, Philip declares that Jesus is the One who was prophesied in the Old Testament, and Nathanael declares that Jesus is the Son of God. All in all, there are five named witnesses who are convinced that Jesus is not merely another prophet. John's narration demonstrates that an encounter with Jesus precipitates a decision about who Jesus is!

John the author reports on these events to build evidence that supports his thesis that "the Word became flesh and [has] made his dwelling among us" (John 1:14). The evidence in his reporting so far relies on what people have seen and heard. At this point, it is foundational, remarkable, and intriguing, but far from conclusive.

John the Baptist's integrity is revealed in his humble commitment to his mission and calling, but he is a relative of Jesus. Andrew was his disciple, but he leaves John to follow Jesus, seemingly with the approval of John. And the first thing Andrew did was to recruit his brother because of what he saw and heard. Philip responded to Jesus' invitation to follow Him, and he recruited Nathanael. All these witnesses change their direction and alliance based on what they have seen and heard from Jesus.

In addition to this *saw* and *said* motif of the first chapter, there is one other motif John is introducing in his reporting. It's the word "believe." John first uses that word in John 1:12:

> Yet to all who *believed* in his name he gave the right to become the children of God.

And at the end of chapter 1, John records Jesus' words to Nathanael:

> You *believe* because I told you I saw you under the fig tree. You shall see greater things than that. (John1:50)

How do you approach belief in the truth of something? What is the evidence you need to identify something as true? Basically, in a court of law a jury must evaluate evidence and minimally determine whether it passes two tests: 1. What was seen by more than one witness? 2. What was said to verify what was seen? However, the integrity of witnesses will be a factor as well.

Take a moment and think about something that you believe. Name that belief. Explain how you came to believe it. What did you hear and see that moved you to believe? Describe how that belief has changed you. Now think through how belief influences identity. If someone asked you the same question the Pharisees asked John, "Who are you?" how would you answer that question? Without hesitation, John answers in John 1:23: "I am the voice of one calling in the desert, 'Make straight the way for the Lord.'" This is a direct quote from the prophecy of Isaiah 40:3. The answer you give to the question "Who are you?" will reflect your beliefs, your identity, and your sense of calling. So who are you?

As we read on in chapters 2 and 3 of the gospel of John, this word "believe" will be repeated frequently.

WISDOM INSIGHT

While truth does not depend on belief to be true, belief is required for recognizing the truth. Something that is true stands on its own, but belief always activates truth through actions that reveal and point to truth.

So what does belief have to do with discerning purpose?

CHAPTER 2 JOHN 1:19–51 STUDY GUIDE

Essential Questions

- Do you believe you were created by God for a purpose? Why, or why not?

- What is the difference between ambition and calling?

Review

- Wisdom—the ability to avoid trouble in a troubled world.
- Proverbs view of godly wisdom—a highway guided by eternal values.
- Jesus Christ is the way, truth, and life (John 14:6; 17:25, 26).

1. Read and discuss John 1:19–51.

- John the Baptist's testimony
  - What words does he use as his testimony?
    - John 1:20

  - Why do you think this is mentioned first?

  - Who are you? (What is your worldview?)
    - What would you say if you were asked that question?

- Have you ever answered that question with an answer about who you are not?

  - Isaiah 40:3—The Pharisees would all know this verse and its context.
    - What was the tone of the Pharisees' response to John's answer?

    - Look at John's response (John 1:26–27).
      - What is the tone of his answer?

  - John 1:28 establishes *a historical location*. Why?

- Sequence of days
  - "The next day" (John 1:29, 35, 43)
    - "The next day" who?
      - John 1:29 _____
      - John 1:35 _____
      - John 1:43 _____
    - Day 1 of sequence
      - What is the repeated verb?

      - What did John say? (John 1:29)

      - (Everyone would know this allusion to Abraham and Isaac's story in Genesis 22.)

    - Day 2 of sequence
      - What is the repeated verb?

- What did John say?

- What happened next?

- What did Andrew say?

- What did Jesus say?

- Day 3 of sequence
  - What is the repeated verb?
  - Dialogue with Nathanael
    - Certainly, there were other dialogues that could have been recorded. Why do you think this one was chosen for this passage?

- Review *saw* and *said* motif.
  - John 1:19–28: (19) testimony; (20) confessed; (21) said, answered; (22) said; (23) replied; (25) questioned; (26) replied

  - John 1:29–34: (29) saw, said; (30) said, (32) testimony, saw; (33) told, see; (34) seen, testify

  - John 1:35–42: (36) saw, said, look; (37) say; (38) saw, asked, said; (39) see, saw; (40) said; (41) tell; (42) said

  - John 1:43–51: (43) said; (44) told; (46) asked, see; (47) saw, said; (48) asked, answered, saw; (49) declared; (50) said, told, saw, see; (51) added, tell, see

- What would you say is the link between seeing and saying?

- John 1:50, "believe."
    - What does it mean to believe?
    - Why is this word appropriate for the end of this recording of the sequence of days?

Belief questions

- What does belief have to do with identity and with calling?

3

SIGN LANGUAGE

(John 2:1–25)

Because we had an early-morning flight out of Boston to Atlanta, we stayed overnight in a hotel just outside of the city of Boston. In the morning, we set aside sufficient time to drop off our rental car and check in well before our flight. I set the GPS for directions to the airport. It was a clear-sky morning as we followed the voice commands for making the right and left turns on our way to the airport. But when we entered the maze of tunnels in Boston, the GPS voice went silent. I had to make a decision just ahead where the tunnel split. There were signs, but neither sign had the word *airport*. I chose the split to the right and immediately realized it was the wrong choice when we came up out of the dark underground into the light of downtown Boston.

No problem. The voice returned, guiding us to make a series of turns that would get us out of downtown. After many time-consuming one-way streets and red lights, my anxiety peaked when we came to a barricade that prevented us from going where we were being instructed to go. After a detour, we found ourselves back on the street we had entered from the tunnel, and I pulled over to figure out what to do.

Time becoming a factor, I spotted a policeman standing a block away. I drove up to him and asked for directions. He explained that the roads were blocked for a road race that morning, but we should drive straight until the end of this street, where we should turn left and look for a sign to the airport. Feeling relieved, we followed his directions and found the sign. However, I missed a turn again because I was in the wrong lane when another sign with the words "Logan Airport," seemed to just pop up at the last minute.

So I went back to relying on the GPS, which brought me onto more Boston city streets instead of the highway toward the airport. Weaving through the streets, we were relieved to see the airport just a few miles away on our right. However, we had to go over a bridge, and when we got to the traffic light where we would turn right to go over the bridge, we saw the bridge begin to move and realized it was a drawbridge. Then we saw a huge container ship crawling toward the bridge at least a mile away.

By this time, totally frustrated and stuck in a bumper-to-bumper traffic jam on the wrong side of the bridge, we watched arriving flights at Logan less than a mile away. The container ship drifted toward the drawbridge while I tried to figure out how to turn around and go a different way. But we were trapped in the middle of an increasing number of cars waiting to cross the bridge, so we had to just sit there and wait. Even after the ship had cleared, the lowering of the bridge seemed to happen in slow motion. Finally, a green light indicated we could cross the bridge. We jockeyed our way to merge along with tens of cars from several different lanes.

Once on the other side of the bridge we spotted clearly marked signs for Logan Airport. After dropping off our rental car, we had an hour to spare before our flight. Phew!

Signs point to a destination. They are not the destination, but they are an important means to an end. However, before a sign becomes an important or helpful means, we have to have a destination in mind. Without a determined destination, a sign may be curious or distracting, but it has little impact. Think of all the signs you ignore on a long trip. On the other hand, businesses like hotels, gas stations, and fast-food restaurants know the power of displaying signs to attract your business as you make your way to your destination. Obviously, signs are useful and essential as guides to a fixed destination. However, sign language can also entice a traveler to forget the destination or pause in their journey to take a detour for attractions and sights along the way.

Throughout the New Testament accounts of Jesus' ministry, it is evident that Jesus is circumspect about performing miraculous signs because people tend to focus on the sign rather than on the destination. John uses the word "sign" for the first time in John 2:11. "This, the first of his miraculous signs, Jesus performed at Cana in Galilee." Because of this first miraculous sign, "his disciples put their faith in [Jesus]" (John 2:11). At the risk of sounding flippant, His disciples seemed to put Jesus in the driver's seat because His miraculous sign seemed to promise fine wine in the journey. However, with the benefit of hindsight, John calls this first miracle a sign that points the disciples to a journey with Jesus to a destination that only He knew.

What was this first miraculous sign? Well, according to John, it happened later on the third day after Jesus' conversation with Nathanael. Jesus and His disciples were attending a wedding when His mother urged Jesus to get involved when the wine prematurely ran out. Somewhat reluctantly, Jesus tells the servants to fill water jars for washing the feet and pour out the water into wine flasks. Miraculously, the water turns to wine, but not just ordinary wine. The host calls this last wine the best wine of the celebration.

John describes this first miracle as a sign that influences Jesus' disciples. What does this sign point to? Like John, we have the benefit of the full story, which allows us to understand that Jesus' miraculous sign language is pointing to the best that was yet to come, and like the almost certainly polluted water that is transformed into fine wine, Jesus will take upon Himself the sins of the world so that we can be transformed into unblemished souls. However, in the moment of that wedding day, it is easy to understand how the new disciples were excited about what the sign meant for them—access to fine wine whenever they were thirsty.

John is not the only writer to refer to signs. Sign language is prevalent throughout Old Testament and New Testament scripture. Matthew records the following brief conversation between Jesus and the Pharisees and Sadducees in Matthew 16:1–4.

> The Pharisees and Sadducees came to Jesus and tested him by asking him to show them a sign from heaven.
> He replied, "When evening comes you say, 'It will be fair weather for the sky is red,' and in the morning, 'Today it will be stormy, for the sky is red and overcast.' You know how to interpret the appearance of the sky, but you cannot interpret the signs of the times. A wicked and adulterous generation looks for a miraculous sign, but none will be given it except the sign of Jonah." Jesus then left them and went away.

The Pharisees and Sadducees knew the story of Jonah who spent three days in the belly of a huge fish. In fact, this is not the only time the religious elite had heard from Jesus about the sign of the prophet Jonah. In Matthew 12:38–41, Jesus taps into the Old Testament story of Jonah to allude to his appointed destination using New Testament sign language.

> Then some of the Pharisees and teachers of the law said to him, "Teacher we want to see a miraculous sign from you."
> He answered, "A wicked and adulterous generation asks for a miraculous sign! But none will be given it except the sign of the prophet Jonah. For as Jonah was three days and three nights in the belly of a huge fish, so the Son of Man will be three days and three nights in the belly of the earth. The men of Nineveh will stand up in judgment with this generation and condemn it; for they repented at the preaching of Jonah, and now one greater than Jonah is here."

The religious elite were enamored with signs rather than what they pointed to. They wanted to see and admire a spectacle. In response, Jesus alludes to the sign of Jonah to point to the ultimate sign of the three-day event of His crucifixion, burial, and resurrection.

Several chapters later in his gospel, John tells the story of Jesus walking on water to rescue the disciples from the rough waters. Rather than emphasizing the miracle, John focuses on the conversation Jesus has with His followers, who were amazed that He was on the other side the next day after that event in John 6:25–34. In this passage, John highlights Jesus' stern warning about focusing on the temporary aspects of sign language instead of on the valuable message the sign conveys. Jesus responds to their questions about how He arrived at this side of the lake, saying, "I tell you the truth, you are looking for me, not because you saw a miraculous sign but because you ate the loaves and had your fill" (John 6:26). In fact, the followers make the same demand that the religious elite had made. "What miraculous sign then will you give that we may see it and believe in you? What will you do? Our forefathers ate the manna in the desert; as it is written: 'He gave them bread from heaven to eat'" (John 6:30, 31). Jesus replies that Moses did not deserve the credit for providing the bread from heaven, "but it is my Father who gives you the bread from heaven. For the bread of God is he who comes down from heaven and gives life to the world" (John 6:32, 33).

Even with this rebuke that points to the destination of the eternal Bread of Life who will sacrifice his life for the world, people were still focused on satisfying their appetite as evidenced by their shortsighted reply: "From now on give us the bread" (John 6:34).

By comparison, the first miraculous sign of turning water into wine has even more potential for focusing on the sign rather than what it points to. Juxtaposed to this remarkable but passively generous first sign, John describes another significant event that happened a few days later when Jesus went up to Jerusalem for the Jewish Passover. When Jesus entered the temple courts and found men selling livestock and exchanging money, He made a whip out of cords and drove them from the temple area.

What a contrast to His first miracle! His first miracle was anonymous, reluctant, and benevolent; but in the next event, John chooses to describe Jesus as aggressive, forceful, and authoritative. In response, the ruling religious elite demand that He provide a miraculous sign to prove that Jesus has the authority to do what He had done (John 2:18). Jesus understands the trap in this demand—they want Jesus to be a magician who adds to His résumé actions that focus on the sign rather than pointing to the destination. So Jesus points to the ultimate miraculous sign of His death and resurrection.

> Destroy this temple, and I will raise it again in three days.
> (John 2:19)

Of course, the Jews do not understand what he is predicting, and His disciples only remember these words: "After he was raised from the dead. Then they believed the Scripture and the words that Jesus had spoken" (John 2:22).

SO WHAT?

Jesus entered history to post His signs at just the right time. Everything He spoke and did pointed to a future when redemption and restoration would be completed.

Imagine what it was like when Jesus walked on earth. Darkness literally and figuratively dominated the world. When the sun set each day, the only light came from candles and lanterns. There were no streetlights, billboards, brightly lit high-rise buildings, spotlights, and neon signs. Additionally, the spoken word was the only source of information. No daily podcasts, news programs, or even newspapers. No television, internet, and radio broadcasts. Few knew how to read the sparse sources of the written word.

As a contemporary of Jesus, the author John recorded the events and words of this extraordinary man who pointed to His death and resurrection that would be a sign for all humankind. So when the Jewish elite demand a sign from Jesus, He points to the ultimate sign—His substitutionary death paying the price for the sins of all humankind and His conquering resurrection over the power of death. This sign has been named the Gospel or Good News for those who receive and believe in the final destination it points to.

But the Pharisees and Sadducees valued the sign instead of the future destination it pointed to.

Two thousand–plus years later, we live in vastly more complicated times inundated with all kinds of information bombarding us through all our senses. Artificial light permeates all but the remotest locations of our world. We have the benefit of completed scripture, as well as historical records. Yet many, like the religious elite of Jesus' time still insist on more evidence, demanding immediate miraculous signs that fulfill temporary desires.

Sign language, like all languages, relies on a vocabulary and gestures that communicate important information for life's journey. We can find comfort, and even delight, in the vocabulary; but like the welcomed sign that pointed my wife and me to Boston's Logan Airport, confirming that we were approaching our destination, the information has a short-lived value because it is not the final destination.

Paul David Tripp, in his book *New Morning Mercies: A Daily Gospel Devotional,* writes about sign language in his May 31 entry:

> The physical world is wonderfully glorious, but it was never meant to be our stopping point any more than the sign that points to something is meant to be the end of the journey. Here's what you and I need to remember about signs. The sign is not the thing; the sign points to the thing. The same can be said of physical creation. It is not the thing that you were made to live for. It was made to point you to the thing you were made to live for, and that thing is God and God alone.

WISDOM INSIGHT

John's Gospel narrative describes Jesus, the embodiment of godly wisdom, performing signs designed for followers then and now to arrive at the correct destination—their redemption and eternal life. As John has indicated in John 1, Jesus' followers must trust the signs, believing in what they point to because believing always leads to action that confirms belief and reveals the truth. Wisdom is always focused on the destination. So John shifts his narration to focus on what it means to believe.

So what role has signs played in your journey so far?

CHAPTER 3 JOHN 2:1–25 STUDY GUIDE

1. **Belief, believer, believe**

    - What is the definition of believe?
        - Religious belief

        - Secular belief

    - What does belief have to do with identity?
        - Examples from John 1
            - John 1:19–23

            - John 1:40–42

            - John 1:4–751

2. **Read John 2:1–11 story #1 (sign language)**

    - Wedding at Cana story (John 2:1–10)
      How do the quoted words below from John 2:11 provide insight to the story?
        - "signs"

        - "revealed"

        - "faith"

3. **Read John 2:12–25 story #2 (sign language)**

    - Jesus clears the temple
        - Contrast this with story #1
            - What is the wedding story about?

- What is the temple story about?

- How did Jesus respond to the Jews?

  ○ Record sign language in the following verses
    - John 2:11
    - John 2:19
    - John 2:22
    - John 2:23
  ○ Identify the key verses about believing in John 2:1–25.

  ○ Write a definition of belief that fits with these verses.

  ○ How does the transitional word "but" provide insight to John 2:24-25?

Where do you see evidence of wisdom in John 2?

Further Thought

Read Mark 9:24. In the light of our discussion about the definitions of belief, what do you think this verse reveals about belief?

ON THE PATHWAY TO BELIEF

(John 3:1–36)

Before we look at perhaps one of the best-known passages of John's Gospel, let's think some more about our essential question: What does it mean to believe?

We live in a time of heightened skepticism. There are so many voices clamoring for our attention. Robo calls invade our cell phones multiple times a day, attempting to scam us into sharing credit card information. Our email boxes daily fill up and overflow with unwanted promotions. Social media posts spread fake news. Television and radio advertising try to convince us that we need their products in order to thrive. In the midst of all these voices, the truth is compromised, becoming relative only to the extent that it works for us or meets our desires at the moment.

However, even though we seemingly live in a time of no absolutes, with untruths swirling around us, we choose to believe in love, goodness, morality, and other values that help define who we are. As a result, what we believe in defines our worldview, and our worldview is confirmed in our actions and our actions determine our pathways in life. Uniquely in all of creation, humans are meaning-makers yearning to know and believe in something that is beyond us.

Those who seek to fool us or take advantage of us know that all humans are meaning-makers. So they appeal to that need by promising that we will have increased worth and purpose if we believe in what they are saying, selling, or promising. They seek to change our values and worldview so that we become lifelong consumers or followers. If we succumb, we become customers who only buy certain brands like Under Armor or Nike, Ford or Chevy, and follow Fox News or CNN. As consumers or customers, what we perceive as truth becomes malleable and transitory to fit our ever-changing desires and perspectives.

Jesus knew this about human nature. John writes:

> Now while he [Jesus] was in Jerusalem at the Passover Feast, many people saw the miraculous signs he was doing and believed in his name. But Jesus would not entrust himself to them, for he knew all men. He did not need man's testimony about man, for he knew what was in man. (John 2:23–25)

Having said this, John then tells the stories of two men who were on a pathway to true belief in John 3:1–6.

Five Steps on the Pathway to Belief
Seek Truth, Test Truth, Believe Truth, Live Truth, Seek Truth
(John 3:1–3)

In chapter 3, John transitions from commenting on Jesus' wisdom about many people to an account of one person, Nicodemus, who was intrigued by what he saw in Jesus. Nicodemus, a Pharisee and a member of the Jewish ruling council, comes to Jesus under the cover of night and said, "Rabbi, we know you are a teacher who has come from God. For no one could perform the miraculous signs you are doing if God were not with him" (John 3:2). In this risky surreptitious night visit, Nicodemus takes the first step toward belief by seeking the truth about this man who "has come from God" (John 3:2). He interprets the sign language correctly by understanding that it is pointing to a commission from God. And by calling Jesus Rabbi, he indicates a humble respect for Jesus' godly authority.

Interestingly, Jesus takes Nicodemus's insightful statement that "no one could perform the miraculous signs ... if God were not with him" and replies by declaring, "I tell you the truth, *no one* can see the kingdom of God unless he is born again" (John 3:3). Thus, Jesus turns Nicodemus's statement about miraculous signs into a statement about what the signs point to—the kingdom of God.

Test Truth (John 3:4–15)

Masterfully, Jesus' statement is a subtle invitation for Nicodemus to respond by testing the truth through clarifying questions: "How can a man be born when he is old?" (John 3:4) and "How can this be?" (John 3:9).

Jesus prefaces His answers to each question by saying, "I tell you the truth" (John 3:5, 3:11) just as He had prefaced His statement in verse 3. By doing so, Jesus is pointing to a capital *T* Truth that is absolute because it comes from God. Once again, He uses the words "no one," meaning absolutely "no one can enter the kingdom of God unless he is born of water and the Spirit" (John 3:5). The implication is that even a well-respected Pharisee and member of the Jewish ruling council cannot enter the kingdom of God based on his résumé, good works, and positions held. Then Jesus defines what it means to be born again. "Flesh gives birth to flesh, but the Spirit gives birth to spirit" (John 3:6). In other words, one does not enter the kingdom of God through effort and achievement. The kingdom of God is activated through a spiritual birth because the kingdom of God is spiritual, not physical.

In response to Nicodemus's incredulity about being born again of the Spirit, Jesus wonders out loud about how Israel's teacher could not understand these things. Then Jesus begins to teach Nicodemus about what it takes to believe the truth.

> "You are Israel's teacher," said Jesus, "and you do not understand these things? I tell you the *truth*, we speak of what we know, and we testify to what we have seen, but you people do not accept our testimony. I have spoken to you of earthly things and you do not *believe*; how then will

you *believe* if I speak of heavenly things? No one has ever gone into heaven except the one who came from heaven—the Son of Man." (John 3:10–13) [Emphasis mine]

(Throughout His lecture, Jesus uses the word "believe" seven times and bookends His message with the word "truth.")

Continuing His response, Jesus cites the example of Moses lifting up an image of a snake in the wilderness as an example of what belief does and how it works. For the contemporary reader, this example may be unclear, but as a Pharisee, Nicodemus would have understood the example perfectly. Because of the nation of Israel's lack of faith in God's leading them to the Promised Land, they became lost in the wilderness and plagued with poisonous snakes. So the people came to Moses, confessed their sin against God, and asked Moses to intercede with God. In response to the people's confession, God instructed Moses to make an image of a snake and put it on a pole, so that when a person was bit by a snake, they were to look at the image of the snake and they would be healed (Num. 21:4–9).

Russell Moore, in his book *The Storm-Tossed Family: How the Cross Reshapes the Home* (Nashville, Tennessee: B&H Publishing Group, 2018), citing Jesus' words in John 3:14–15, describes belief as looking "to that which frightens us most, to that which exposes us for who we really are, in all our sin and all our brokenness" (p. 263). Basic belief requires a recognition that motivates a focus on that which you believe. Whatever you say you believe must command your full attention. According to scripture, what you focus on, where you look, and what you look at, will reveal your heart's real focus.

> I lift up my eyes to you, to you whose throne is in heaven. As the eyes of slaves look to the hand of their master, as the eyes of a maid look to the hand of her mistress, so our eyes look to the LORD our God till he shows his mercy. (Ps. 123:1)

> But my eyes are fixed on you O Sovereign LORD; in you I take refuge -- do not give me over to death. (Ps. 141:8)

As a scholar who knew this Exodus story, Nicodemus would recognize that the analogy of Moses lifting up the snake in the desert portrayed true belief in God's provision of relief, healing, and rescue. So when Jesus declared, "just as Moses lifted up the snake in the desert, so the Son of Man must be lifted up, that everyone who believes in him may have eternal life" (John 3:14). Nicodemus understood that Jesus was providing a clear explanation of the need for a spiritual rebirth that begins with believing in a future sign that Jesus would fulfill.

Believe Truth
(John 3:16–21)

Testing, understanding, and recognizing the truth of an analogy is a step toward belief, just as Nicodemus took steps toward meeting with Jesus is evidence of a mind open to asking questions about His identity and purpose. However, belief is not solely an intellectual acknowledgment of something that makes sense. So Jesus continues His lecture about the need to actively believe.

Jesus tells Nicodemus that belief comes alive when it is centered on the person of God's one and only Son, "that whoever believes in him shall not perish but have eternal life" (John 3:16). And, "Whoever believes in him is not condemned, but whoever does not believe stands condemned already because he has not believed in the name of God's one and only Son" (John 3:18). These words are understood in the light of the analogy of the snake-bitten Israelites being saved by believing that looking up at the snake would heal them. If they refused to look at the image of the snake, they were condemned to die. Looking is an act of faith just as believing in Jesus is an act of faith. Just as for the Israelites nothing more was required than to look and be healed, nothing more is required than believing in God's one and only Son for redemption.

The author of Hebrews follows up his chapter on faith with the following proclamation: Let us fix our eyes on Jesus, the author and perfecter of our faith, who for the joy set before Him endured the cross, scorning its shame, and sat down at the right hand of the throne of God (Heb. 12:2).

Believing is fixing our eyes on the One who was lifted up on a criminal's cross on our behalf.

Jesus finishes His instruction, telling Nicodemus that "everyone who does evil hates the light and will not come into the light … But whoever lives by the truth comes into the light, so that it may be seen plainly that what he has done has been done through God" (John 3:20, 3:21). This conclusion is both a warning and an invitation for and to Nicodemus to carefully consider the truth in the light of His signs and instructions. It is also a definition of what it looks like to believe—belief demands an active step from a willful ignorance into the acknowledgment of the truth.

Live Truth
(John 3:22–36)

And somewhat abruptly, John shifts from the interview with Nicodemus to an account of John the Baptist. The vivid scene of Nicodemus's night encounter with Jesus is just dropped by John the author. It becomes clear that he has a purpose in this shift, using the words "After this, Jesus and His disciples went out into the Judean countryside, where he spent some time with them, and baptized" (John 3:22). John moves on to report on the impact of Jesus' ministry—more and more people were coming to Jesus to be baptized. As a result, John's disciples came to him reporting that everyone is going to Jesus evoking John's remarkably humble response:

> A man can receive only what is given him from heaven. You yourselves can testify that I said. 'I am not the Christ but am sent ahead of him.' The bride belongs to the bridegroom. The friend who attends the bridegroom waits and listens for him, and is full of joy when he hears the bridegroom's voice. That joy is mine, and it is now complete. *He must become greater, I must become less.* [My emphasis.]
> The one who comes from above is above all; the one who is from the earth belongs to the earth, and speaks as from the earth. The one who comes from heaven is above all. He testifies to what he has seen and heard, but no one accepts

> his testimony. The man who has accepted it has certified that God is truthful ... Whoever believes in the Son has eternal life, but whoever rejects the Son will not see life, for God's wrath remains on him. (John 3:27–33, 3:36)

By shifting the focus from Nicodemus to John the Baptist, John demonstrates that belief is not belief without living out the ramifications of what you say you believe. As we will see in the next chapter and from this point on in John's Gospel, true belief is always demonstrated through the actions of the believer. John's famous words, "He must become greater, I must become less" (John 3:30), is a remarkable act and testimony that verifies what it means to truly believe.

In fact, later in his gospel, John subtly verifies this all-important theme about belief when he writes about the Pharisees' rebuke of the temple guards when they didn't arrest Jesus (John 7:45–50), reporting that Nicodemus stood up for Jesus—a risky action. And again, after the crucifixion of Jesus, John tells us that Nicodemus joined Joseph of Arimathea, asking for the body of Jesus, contributing about seventy pounds of myrrh and aloes for embalming the body (John 19:39). In each passage, John reminds readers about who Nicodemus was: "Nicodemus, who had come to Jesus earlier" (John 7:50) and "Nicodemus, the man who earlier visited Jesus at night" (John 9:39). In both scenarios, Nicodemus takes a risk when he chooses to speak out and step out from what was expected by those who did not believe in Jesus.

In his statement of the purpose for writing his gospel of Jesus Christ, John verifies this theme that belief is only truly belief when it is acted upon.

> Jesus did many other miraculous signs in the presence of his disciples, which are not recorded in this book. But these are written that you may *believe* that Jesus is the Christ, the Son of God, and that by *believing* you may have life in his name. (John 20:30, 20:31; emphasis mine)

SO WHAT?

So what does it mean to believe? There was a reason and purpose for Jesus' ministry lasting three years. Jesus' patient public ministry demonstrated that to believe requires a process that begins with an uncompromising search for truth, continued by a thorough testing of truth, followed by acknowledging truth, and completed by acting according to that truth. Over a three-year period, He repeatedly called His disciples to seek, test, believe, and live truth. The obedient sacrificial laying down of His life on a criminal's cross provided the ultimate lesson for His disciples about what it means to believe.

Two curious events in Jesus' ministry inform our understanding of how becoming a believer is a process. Mark, Matthew, and Luke all report these two events in their gospel accounts. The first event is the transfiguration of Jesus. Peter, James, and John accompanied Jesus on a hike up a high mountain where they witnessed Jesus transfigured in "dazzling white clothes" and Elijah and Moses appeared before them (Mark 9:2–4). Jesus instructed them not to tell anyone about this event "until the Son of Man had risen from the dead. [So] they kept the matter to themselves, discussing what 'rising from the dead' meant" (Mark 9:9, 9:10). All three authors also report on the second event following right after the transfiguration when Jesus, with Peter, James, and John encounter a large crowd gathered around the other disciples. However, only Mark records the full conversation between Jesus and a man who had brought his son to the disciples for healing.

> What are you arguing with them about? he [Jesus] asked. A man in the crowd answered, "Teacher, I brought my son, who is possessed by a spirit that has robbed him of speech. Whenever it seizes him, it throws him to the ground. He foams at the mouth, gnashes his teeth and becomes rigid. I asked your disciples to drive out the spirit, but they could not."
> "O *unbelieving* generation," Jesus replied, "how long shall I stay with you? How long shall I put up with you? Bring the boy to me."

> So they brought him, When the spirit saw Jesus, it immediately threw the boy into a convulsion. He fell to the ground and rolled around, foaming at the mouth.
> Jesus asked the boy's father, "How long has he been like this?"
> "From childhood," he answered. "It has often thrown him into fire or water to kill him. But if you can do anything, take pity on us and help us."
> "If you can?" said Jesus. "Everything is possible for him who *believes*."
> Immediately the boy's father exclaimed, "I do *believe*; help me overcome my *unbelief*!" (Mark 9:16–24, emphasis mine)

The disciples and the father are in the process of encountering divine truth and belief. Peter, James, and John find themselves testing what they saw and heard on the mountain by asking what it means. Meanwhile, the other disciples attempt to heal the demon-possessed boy unsuccessfully because of their unbelief. And it is the father of the boy that acknowledges that he believes the truth but he needs help in his unbelief. Jesus honors the father's belief despite his unbelief.

WISDOM INSIGHT

At this point in their faith journey, the disciples were double-minded in their effort to heal the boy while the father was single-minded in his pursuit of Jesus. Do you identify with the father? Do you find yourself in the brokenness and troubles of our world believing that God can work but still needing help in your unbelief? If so, you are in a process that God understands. It is OK to acknowledge your unbelief as you humbly doubt yourself. However, doubting the Almighty God and hedging your trust in Him by also trusting in yourself is double-minded and unstable. In other words, we are being truthful and yet single-minded when we confess our inadequacy, but we are being double-minded and unstable when we ask God for His intervention as a backup strategy while we trust in our own efforts. The disciples tried in their own strength and assumptions about

So What Wisdom

their status as disciples to heal the boy and were miserable failures, but these same disciples became world-changing healers and proclaimers after the resurrection because they believed Jesus' promises of eternal life. You and I have those same promises, as well as the full revelation of God in scripture enabling us to seek, test, believe, and live the truth.

CHAPTER 4 JOHN 3:1–36 STUDY GUIDE

1. **Belief**
   - Why does Jesus affirm the father's imperfect belief? (Mark 9:24)

   - What does Jesus know about "all men"? (John 2:24, 2:25)

2. **Word searches**
   (Scan John 3:1–21 and list the verses that contain the following words.)
   - Truth

   - Know/see or seen

   - Believe

3. **Read John 3:1–21**
   - Outline
   John 3:1–3 Nicodemus: Seeker of Truth

   John 3:4–9 Nicodemus: Tester of Truth

   John 3:10–21 Jesus: Speaker of Truth

   - What does Jesus say about understanding truth?

- What is the evidence of accepting truth?

4. **Read John 3:22–36 (Coming into the light)**
   - Why does John follow the story about Nicodemus with John the Baptist's testimony about Jesus? (Hint: How is this section an example of John 3:1–21?)

5. **Further thought**
   Solomon, in his first nine chapters of Proverbs, highlighted four heart preferences that are evidence of the heart of wisdom.

   - Reverence for God's authority instead of personal autonomy (Proverbs 1:7, 9:10)
   - Rejection of sinners' enticements (Proverbs 1:10, 1:15)
   - Preference for sound judgment and discernment (Proverbs 3:10)
   - Deference for humility (Proverbs 6:3)

   Based on these four dispositions, how does John the Baptist measure up? How do you measure up? (Note: It is about choices, not performance!)

6. Two other passages to contemplate

   Jeremiah 9:23–24
   1 Corinthians 1:20–31

   - How do these verses further your thoughts about our study of John 3?

Where are you on the highway to gospel wisdom: seek Truth, test Truth, believe Truth, live Truth?

5

A SAMARITAN WOMAN'S BELIEF

(John 4:1–42)

John furthers his theme about what it means to truly believe in his next account about Jesus' encounter with a Samaritan woman. On His way to Galilee, He chooses to pass through Samaria, deciding to stop at a well in a town called Sychar. John provides a lot of details about what happens at the well, including the specific place—Jacob's well—and the time, which was noon. Journalistic details that authenticate the ensuing report. In the telling of this event, John makes it clear that this is a highly unusual encounter—a single Samaritan woman approached by a single Jewish man. "For Jews do not associate with Samaritans" (John 4:9).

Shocked that Jesus asked her to draw water for Him, the woman responds, "You are a Jew and I am a Samaritan woman. How can you ask me for a drink?" (John 4:9). Just as He did with Nicodemus, Jesus answers her question with an unexpected metaphysical statement. "If you knew the gift of God and who it is that asks you for a drink, you would have asked him and he would have given you living water" (John 4:10). Of course, this statement encourages questions from the woman who seeks to know and understand more about this Jewish man who has moved toward her instead of away from her. She asks, "Where can you get this living water?" (4:11), and "Are you greater than our father Jacob, who gave us this well and drank from it himself, as did his sons and his flocks and herds?" (John 4:12).

By asking questions, the woman expresses incredulity while at the same time opening the door for her to test the truth of what Jesus is saying. Jesus answers her questions, pointing out that there are two kinds of water—the water from the well that will only quench thirst temporarily and the water He gives that "will become … a spring of water welling up to eternal life" (John 4:14). Her response is reminiscent of Nicodemus's misunderstanding of Jesus' figurative language. "The woman said to him, 'Sir give me this water so that I won't get thirsty and have to keep coming here to draw water'" (John 4:15). In both situations—Nicodemus and the Samaritan woman—Jesus uses a figure of speech that provides an opportunity for continuing the conversation. For the Pharisee Nicodemus, Jesus uses an allusion to the story of Moses, fashioning an image of a snake in the wilderness to challenge Nicodemus to connect his Old Testament knowledge to a future lifting up of Jesus on the cross. On the other hand, for the Samaritan woman, he uses the image of "a spring of water welling up to eternal life" to get her to connect her need for clean water from the well to her need for eternal life.

Masterfully, Jesus shifts the conversation, telling her to get her husband and come back. When she truthfully admits that she has no husband, "Jesus said to her, 'You are right when you say you have no husband. The fact is, you have had five husbands, and the man you now have is not your husband. What you say is quite true'" (John 4:17, 4:18). Jesus is bluntly literal about how her life is a mess! Even in our contemporary secular culture, she would be viewed as troubled. In that culture, she would be viewed as an immoral outcast. Perhaps that is why she is at the well in the middle of the day instead of early morning when others would have gone to the well.

However, she does not recoil in shame. Rather, she shifts the conversation to the disagreement between Samaritans and Jews about where to worship. Jesus responds, saying "Believe me," followed by an explanation of true worship and belief that has nothing to do with a geographical location. "Yet a time is coming and has now come when true worshipers will worship the Father in spirit and *truth*, for they are the kind of worshipers the

Father seeks. God is spirit and his worshipers must worship in spirit and in *truth*" (John 4:23, 4:24, emphasis mine). Notice the emphasis on truth and what is true throughout this conversation. Jesus is patiently leading this woman through a belief process inviting her to seek and test truth through questions and dialogue. When she states what she believes about the Messiah in verse 25, Jesus declares, "I who speak to you am he." Quite a remarkable statement, considering He did not reveal this to Nicodemus or His disciples at this point in His ministry.

The woman, apparently overwhelmed by what she just heard, leaves her water jar and goes back to town inviting people to "Come see a man who told me everything I ever did. Could this be the Christ?" (John 4:29). Because of her testimony, "many of the Samaritans from that town believed in him" (John 4:39).

> So when the Samaritans came to him, they urged him to stay with them, and he stayed two days. And because of his words many more became believers. (John 4:40-41)

What an amazing blessing this town experienced—two entire days of listening to the Savior of the world! And this all became possible through the words of an immoral woman!

SO WHAT?

In this longest recorded conversation between Jesus and anyone else in the gospels, there are a number of important insights about Jesus, His ministry, and its impact. John's purposeful recording of Jesus' conversation with Nicodemus followed by his recording of Jesus' conversation with the woman provides a contrast that demonstrates that Jesus came to reach all kinds of people. The woman's immediate response and testimony contrasts with Nicodemus's delayed response demonstrating that the process of belief can be immediate or in the future.

Meanwhile, the disciples of Jesus remain clueless. They wonder why Jesus is talking to a woman. But no one asked, "What do you want?"

Or "Why are you talking with her?" Instead, by urging him to eat something, they focus on Jesus' physical needs, completely out of sync with what he had been doing. When Jesus replies, "I have food to eat that you know nothing about" (John 4:32). They only think literally about who might have brought Him food. Jesus then needs to explain that his food "is to do the will of Him who sent [Him] and to finish his work" (John 4:34). Then Jesus patiently explains the mission through the metaphor of reaping a harvest, suggesting that the disciples will have a part in harvesting what others have sown. This teaching is in itself a sowing of seed that will bear fruit after His resurrection and continues to be relevant to this day.

In his gospel of Jesus, John shows us that Jesus always moves toward those who are seeking Truth by inviting them to walk on the pathway to seek, test, believe, and live Truth. At this point in our study, there is increasing evidence that belief is not a one-time event; it is an ongoing process that seeks, tests, believes, and lives out the truth as we grow in our understanding and knowledge of Jesus the embodiment of godly wisdom. This is what Solomon was pointing to when he wrote, "The fear of the LORD is the *beginning* of wisdom and the knowledge of the Holy One is understanding" (Prov. 9:10, emphasis mine). A "*beginning*" suggests a start that leads to a way to an end.

So what does all this have to do with you and me? What is the application I can make that confirms that I am a believer in Jesus? So far in our study, we have been introduced to a variety of people: John the Baptist, who is single-minded about preparing the way for Jesus; the Pharisees who are concerned about following the law to justify their superior status; the disciples who choose to follow Jesus; Nicodemus who cautiously seeks to understand who Jesus is; and a Samaritan woman who recognizes her need for the Messiah and who verifies her belief in him by proclaiming the news to all around her. Where do I fit on this list? Am I a committed believer who is single-minded about pointing to Jesus? Or, am I more like a religiously obedient adherent to the rules and expectations of a Christian institution? Or, am I a follower of Jesus anxious to know him? Or, am I a seeker who is surreptitiously exploring what it would mean to be a believer?

Or, am I a sinner who has no claim to godliness but knows my need for a Savior?

My answer to these questions reveals where I am on the pathway to Truth. The good news is that Jesus always moves toward me patiently calling me to believe that Jesus is the way, Truth and life.

CHAPTER 5 JOHN 4:1-42 STUDY GUIDE

1. Review
   - Seek Truth—Test Truth—Believe Truth—Live Truth
     - What do you think gets in the way of daily walking on this pathway?

   - Read Jeremiah 9:23–24
     - "let him boast about this: that he understands and knows me"
     - Godly wisdom is about understanding and knowing the LORD.
   - Read 1 Corinthians 1:20–31
     - Worldly wisdom does not know and understand God.
     - "Christ the wisdom of God" is the embodiment of "wisdom that came from God."
   - Read the following "looking" verses:
     - Psalm 123:1, 141:8; Proverbs 17:24; Hebrew 12:2

2. Read John 4:1–26 about the Samaritan woman.
   - Note that Jesus moves away from baptizing people. His disciples are doing that, but His mission is not about baptizing people. He moves toward his mission and toward those who need the Truth.
   - Jesus moves toward, not away, from the Samaritan woman
     - Compare the Samaritan woman passage to the Nicodemus passage, and add to the partial list below.
       - Differences
         - Nicodemus initiates the conversation while it is Jesus that initiates the conversation with the woman.
         - Nicodemus is a highly respected religious leader. The woman is a sinner. What does that indicate about Jesus' mission?

- Similarities
  - Jesus' answers are about spiritual truths.
  - Jesus knows both of them.
  - Both see Jesus as a prophet.

○ How does the woman test the truth?

○ At what point does the truth become important? (John 4:17, 4:18)
  - Truth becomes important when it becomes personal. Explain.

○ Copy each phrase that includes the vocabulary in John 4: 21–24
  - Believe

  - True

  - Truth

○ John 4:5–26 Jesus declares the truth that he is the Messiah for the first time.
  - John 8:24—*What is the truth Jesus declares in this verse?*

3. Read John 4:27–38. about the Disciples Perspective
   - What are the disciples focused on?

   - What is Jesus' focus?

   - Do you identify? Are there moments in your life when you are focused on temporal/physical realities that rob you of your godly wisdom and mission focus? Give one example.

4. Read John 4:39–42 about the Samaritan's Perspective
   - Why did many Samaritans believe?

   - What two kinds of belief are portrayed? (Hint: Belief is not all or nothing.)

   - According to these verses, what does it take to grow in belief?

5. Applications: *These questions are asking you to recall the faith/belief journey you have been on. As you answer, think about the pathway for attaining wisdom that is at the beginning of this study.*
   - When and why did you first believe in Jesus?

- How has your perspective changed over time?

- What does all this have to do with wisdom? (Jer. 9:24)

6

A ROYAL OFFICIAL BELIEVES

John 4:43–54

After two days of teaching in Samaria Jesus continued His journey to Galilee knowing full well "that a prophet has no honor in his own country" (John 4:43). Nevertheless, Jesus' mission was to give Himself to those who would demand His life. Ironically, He left Samaria where many believed that He was the Savior they were looking for to go to Galilee, where the people welcomed Him just to see more miraculous signs like the ones He performed at the Passover Feast.

In Cana where He had turned the water into wine, He met "a certain royal official whose son lay sick at Capernaum" (John 4:46). The royal official humbled himself despite his rank and position, begging Jesus to heal his son. There must have been a buzz in the crowd when they overheard the royal official begging Jesus to come home with him so that Jesus would save his son. Shockingly, Jesus responds with a stern rebuke: "Unless you people see miraculous signs and wonders … you will never believe" (John 4:48).

We tend to stereotype Jesus as a gentle servant who defers to compassion rather than rebuke. However, in almost every instance, John describes Jesus as a teacher who practices uncompromising tough love, willing to confront falsehood and hypocrisy. If you have a Bible in which all Jesus' quotes are written in red, you can quickly survey how often Jesus is seriously intentional in his words, confronting unbelief and challenging those who approach him. For example, reread John 1:37–38, 1:50; 2:4, 2:16; 3:10; 4:17–18, 4:32. In all these examples, Jesus speaks with authority, challenging the assumptions of those around him while always pointing to Truth.

So when Jesus responds to the royal official by saying, "Unless *you people* see miraculous signs and wonders, you will never believe" (John 4:48, emphasis mine), Jesus is really addressing all those who are gathering around the royal official hoping to see another miracle.

I love watching magicians perform their tricks, deceptions, and illusions. The best magicians cause us to wonder about their magic. Magicians fill Las Vegas auditoriums with admirers wanting to be thrilled by their incredible feats. However, every magician knowing that they need to draw people into their act will rehearse over and over their art of deception, providing elaborate distractions and manipulations for the sake of a successful magic act. Their only promise is to entertain by drawing attention to their skills. The magic is just an end in itself. Consequently, there is no other benefit except the entertainment and thrill of the performance.

So when the crowd begins to buzz about the potential of another magical sign, Jesus does the opposite of what any magician would do. He downplays the sign and rebukes the crowd for their shallow demands for another spectacle. In this incident, like others, Jesus' message is about believing in Him as the Savior of the world, not His signs and miracles, because these actions are just signs that point to a destination—Calvary and an empty tomb.

The good news of this passage about the royal official is that Jesus does not walk away from the royal official after His rebuke. When the official responds by respectfully and simply asking Jesus to come home with him, Jesus makes a brief, simple statement ignoring the royal official's request. The father has a choice—to believe Jesus or demand that Jesus come with him. He chose to take Jesus at his word. He did not demand a sign, and he did not protest; instead, he stepped out in faith, illustrating a living example of what it means to believe in Jesus. He trusts Jesus to heal his son's fever and immediately turned toward home. On his way home, he received word that his son's fever had left him at exactly the time Jesus had said his son would live. The official's belief, like the Samaritan woman's belief, was not in a sign, but in the word of the LORD. As a result, in each case their faith affects others. Many Samaritans believe, and the official's entire family and servants become believers.

SO WHAT?

So what does this have to do with me? Well, how do I approach Jesus in my life's circumstances?

- Do I approach Him in prayer demanding outcomes and begging Him to solve my problems?
- When inevitable trouble and brokenness rob me of my comfort, do I demand that Jesus perform a miracle for me?
- Do I treat prayer as a customer service complaint center?
- What percentage of my prayer time is dedicated to considering my role in God's redemptive plan in comparison to listing all my requests?
- Do my words of prayer reveal my trust in God's word and a willingness to live out that trust?

WISDOM INSIGHT

When, like the royal official and the Samaritan woman, I single-mindedly trust in the Lord and do not scheme to get my way because of my limited understanding of my world and God's purposes, and when I approach God in prayer acknowledging and desiring His redemptive plan for me, my family, and those in my sphere of influence, I am empowering life-saving belief that impacts not just me but many others.

In Proverbs 9, Solomon creates a scenario where Lady Wisdom and Lady Folly both issue invitations to a feast. Both invitations offer food, drink, and promises. Lady Folly, with salacious innuendo, promises the opportunity to drink sweet stolen water and to eat secret delicious food. On the other hand, in addition to a carefully planned full banquet of prepared meats and fine wine, Lady Wisdom offers a relationship that promises, "Through me your days will be many and years will be added to your life" (Prov. 9:11). Likewise, our contemporary world offers seductive promises that appeal to our physical and psychological desires, but like those who chose Lady Folly's invitation "little do [we] know that the dead are there, that her guests are in the depths of the grave" (Prov. 9:18). However, John's Gospel provides good news that through Jesus' redemptive death and resurrection, we can experience the banquet of eternal life when we choose His invitation to believe in His name. Godly wisdom has a verifiable name and historical event that we can believe and trust in—Jesus Christ, crucified and resurrected. And when we live out our belief in tangible ways, others around us are influenced to believe.

So what are some evidences you can cite that indicate your faith has influenced those in your sphere of influence?

CHAPTER 6 JOHN 4:43–54 STUDY GUIDE

1. **Read John 4:43–54.**
   - Why do you think Jesus makes the distinction between seeing miraculous signs and believing? How is seeing different from believing?

   - What attitude is portrayed by the royal official's statement? Why does Jesus respond so positively to him?

   - How is this evidence of belief?

   - What is the result of acting on Jesus' words that lead to the entire household believing?

2. **Application**

   The story: A royal official is single-minded in seeking Jesus, compelled by his son's illness. He requests that Jesus come with him before his son dies. Jesus tells him his son will live. The royal official tests Jesus' promise by making his way home without him. His son is healed, and the whole household believes.

   - How has this played out in your life? When did you take a step of faith that led to a deeper faith and recognition of truth you would have never obtained? Give an example.

7

GODLY WISDOM IS GOSPEL WISDOM

When Solomon writes at the conclusion of his curriculum about godly wisdom, "The fear of the LORD is the beginning of wisdom, and knowledge of the Holy One is understanding" (Prov. 9:10), he is pointing to Jesus, the "Holy One" who came "and made his dwelling among us" (John 1:14), so that "by believing [in Him] you may have life in Him" (John 20:31). In Solomon's curriculum, godly wisdom is personified in Lady Wisdom, and Solomon teaches that gaining wisdom begins with a relationship with Lady Wisdom. John's Gospel teaches that godly wisdom has a historical name—Jesus Christ—and is attained and completed by revering and believing in Him. Both writers argue that the way of godly wisdom leads to a flourishing abundant life. John's Gospel completes what Solomon in Proverbs 1–9 point to about how life-giving right living defeats the destructive chains of the self-seeking gratification of temporary desires. But living wisely is not about following rules and striving to be perfect. John's narrative teaches that godly wisdom is found in a relationship with Jesus, and in his gospel of Jesus, John invites his readers to believe in Jesus' name and His life-giving offer to become children of God.

In the conclusion of my first book *A Complete Guide to Godly Wisdom*, I wrote,

> Solomon's proverbs about godly wisdom promise eternal value if one chooses to build his/her life on the foundation of eternal values and the pursuit of knowing God. And

that promise is brought to fulfillment in the person of Jesus Christ.

> It is because of him [God] that you are in Christ Jesus, who has become for us the *wisdom* of God—that is our righteousness, holiness, and redemption.
> (1 Cor. 1:30, emphasis mine)

In the Old Covenant, godly wisdom provides a pathway for revering God. It proposed a (path) way of living according to wisdom and truth. Lady Wisdom declares in Proverbs 8:20–31:

> I walk in the way of righteousness, along the paths of justice bestowing a rich inheritance on those who love me and making their treasuries full.

Her offer to the reader of Proverbs is "a rich inheritance on those who love" her. Ultimately, becoming wise is about a loving relationship instead of following rules ... And Jesus declares in John 14:6:

> I am the way and the truth and the life. No one comes to the Father except through me.

Before the New Covenant was established by Jesus Christ, Lady Wisdom in Proverbs provided a personification of godly wisdom and a foreshadowing of the Messiah who would become the wisdom of God for eternal righteousness, holiness, and redemption.

Solomon's precepts for wisely avoiding the pitfalls of a troubled world are the blueprint for John's Gospel of Jesus' perfect life, sacrificial death, and victorious resurrection. John's Gospel portrays Jesus as the embodiment of godly wisdom: "In Him was life, and that life was the light of men" (John 1:4), and whoever finds Him and believes in Him gains "the right to become children of God" (John 1:12). Godly wisdom has a name—Jesus

Christ! While Solomon wrote about the beginning of wisdom, John testifies that the completion of wisdom is knowledge of and a relationship with the Holy One. Godly wisdom becomes gospel wisdom when you attain and experience godly wisdom through knowing and believing in Jesus.

Paul David Tripp writes in his daily gospel devotional book *New Morning Mercies* (Crossway, 2014):

> The apostle Peter encourages people to live in a radical new way because they have been given "all things that pertain to life and godliness" (2 Pet. 1:3). So you and I aren't left to our own maturity, character, ingenuity, righteousness, wisdom, or power. Not only that, but the gospel redefines how we understand the human struggle, where we get our identity, where we look for peace and security, what we consider in life to be dangerous, what we see as successful living, and so on. It is true that when Jesus takes up residence in us, everything in life changes. Nothing remains the same. (August 18 entry)

John's Gospel was written to invite you to become a child of God by believing in and following "the Holy One." By telling the story of Jesus' last three years of his life, beginning with his baptism and ending with his crucifixion and resurrection, John points his readers to the wisdom of the life-giving gospel.

Let's review the big ideas from John's first four chapters:

- John's Gospel theme: All who believe in Jesus have the right to be born from above as children of God.
- Believing is responding and acting on God's calling, and calling is confirmed through belief, while belief is confirmed through one's actions. In the first four chapters, we see this theme portrayed by
    - John the Baptist as a voice calling in the wilderness
    - the disciples who choose to follow Jesus
    - Nicodemus who approaches belief by seeking truth

- o the Pharisees who work against Jesus' call to believe
  - o the Samaritan woman who believes in Jesus and calls an entire town to belief
  - o the royal official who believes and trusts in Jesus' word influencing his entire family to become believers
- Humility is a mark of calling and belief
  - o John the Baptist chooses to edify Jesus rather than himself.
  - o Jesus points away from his miracles to his obedient sacrificial death on the cross.
  - o The disciples leave their vocation and families to serve Jesus.
  - o The Samaritan woman confesses her sins and calls others to belief.
  - o The royal official submits to Jesus instead of pulling rank and insisting on Jesus coming home with him.
- Sign language—all pathways make use of sign language that points the way to a destination. Recognizing the "highway" signs and their significance requires wisdom, understanding, and knowledge.
- Discovering or uncovering the truth is the highway that leads to eternal life
  - o Seek to know truth.
  - o Test truth.
  - o Believe in truth.
  - o Verify truth by living out truth.

Solomon's precepts for the beginning of godly wisdom pointed to a pathway that led to knowledge, understanding, prudence, discernment, humility, and a long life. John's Gospel portrays the completion of godly wisdom as a pathway that leads to Jesus, "the way, the truth and the [eternal] life" that we all yearn for.

Godly wisdom cannot be attained without knowing and understanding God. The pathway of godly wisdom leads us into a relationship that reveres God through following his precepts that lead to the ultimate destination of a restored relationship with God through Jesus Christ. On that pathway, we pass from darkness to light by seeking truth, testing truth, believing truth, and living in truth. Ultimately, godly wisdom is about an intimate relationship with our Creator and Savior who intends the best for you, not just for you but also through you for those in your spheres of influence.

PART II

JAMES'S GODLY WISDOM INSTRUCTIONS FOR LIVING OUT THE GOSPEL IN A POST-RESURRECTION WORLD

8

SINGLE-MINDED FAITH

James 1:2–18

In part II, we transition from the first four chapters of John's Gospel to James's letter "to the twelve tribes scattered among the nations." However, in making this transition, I am not suggesting that the rest of John's Gospel of Jesus Christ is not worth reading and studying. John artfully records Jesus' ministry, words, and actions, developing his theme about what it means to believe, and "by believing you may have life in His name" (John 20:31). That life is the same life that Solomon alludes to in his conclusion of the godly wisdom curriculum, pointing to how one who has godly wisdom will choose a life of pursuing eternal values over worldly values. But questions remain: What does godly wisdom look like in our post-resurrection world? What are the practical behaviors that mark and confirm our belief in the embodiment of godly wisdom—Jesus Christ, the Son of God?

James's letter can be seen as the New Testament extension of Solomon's teaching about how godly wisdom increases knowledge of God. In the same way, Solomon taught seventeen godly wisdom "my son" precepts, James highlights eight "my brothers" exhortations for what godly wisdom should look like for believers in a post-resurrection world.

Multiple times in his daily gospel devotional *New Morning Mercies*, Paul David Tripp states that we are living "between the 'already' and the 'not yet.'" In his October 9 devotional, he quotes Paul's well-known "armor of God" passage found in Ephesians 6:10–18. Then he asks and answers a question about what it really means to live between the "already" and the "not yet" of our post-resurrection world.

> Why does Paul end his letter to the Ephesians in this way? He does so because he understands that on this side of forever, life is war. When he tells his readers to put on gospel armor and get ready for war, Paul is not introducing a new topic; no, he's summarizing everything he's said so far … What is this war about? It is the great war for the rulership of our hearts … We are tempted to have more excitement in the things of this world, than we do with the reality that we have become the children of God.

Where the apostle Paul uses figurative language about donning "the full armor of God" in preparation for what Tripp describes as "the great war for the rulership of our hearts," James provides believers with straightforward literal instructions for how we are to wisely fight the good fight for the rulership of our hearts. Each of the eight instructions we find in James's letter is about prudently discerning what it takes to win the war for who rules our hearts.

"My brothers" Exhortation #1: Post-resurrection wisdom is exhibited through single-minded perseverance.

After introducing himself as "a servant of God and the Lord Jesus Christ," James writes this astonishing sentence: "Consider it pure joy, my brothers, whenever you face trials of many kinds," declaring that the first mark of post-resurrection godly wisdom—an attitude of pure joy when faced with the inevitable troubles and temptations of this world. James instructs his brothers in Christ to consider it a joy to experience "trials of many kinds." But he does not put a period on this thought without explaining why: "because you know that the testing of your faith develops perseverance" (James 1:2, 1:3).

Why do we need to know this? Perseverance is a necessary disposition for survival in war. The kind of joy James is talking about is connected to perseverance because perseverance is an eternal value that produces mature knowledge and understanding of how worldly hardships are temporary and momentary when we view them from an eternal perspective. Practically speaking, in our imperfect world, perseverance leads to maturity. We know this truth through everyday life experiences. Whether it is choosing the pains of disciplining our bodily desires within our goal of being fit, or when we have no choice but to persevere through an illness or a conflict, we know instinctively that perseverance is necessary for a mature perspective. However, James points to a supernatural joyful eternal perspective despite painful trials and troubles. This is a "pure joy" (James 1:2), not dependent on good things to happen, but because we know the big picture that our pain and suffering is momentary in the light of eternity. James, the brother of Jesus, knew this truth firsthand because he witnessed Jesus' perseverance in enduring horrible suffering on the cross that led to his awesome resurrection by conquering death.

James is pointing out that godly wisdom always looks beyond the moment to a fulfillment of God's perfect will because Jesus modeled how we can become someone who perseveres in the midst of dire trouble, by exercising firm faith while knowing that the end result will be an eternal blessing. Sam Allberry writes in his book *James for You*:

> Notice James says, "Consider." He is not telling us so much how to feel, as he is telling us how to think. He is not saying *Pretend this is fun*. Nor is he calling us always to have a sickly grin or stiff upper lip. No, James is telling us to think about our trials in a certain way. There is a point of view we need to adopt a particular way to consider what is going on. (p.13)

As Allberry points out, the big idea of this first exhortation is the importance of developing mature perseverance and a single-minded faith because "blessed is the man who perseveres under trial, because when he has stood the test, he will receive the crown of life that God has promised to those who love Him" (James 1:12). One who is truly wise is able to consider trials of many kinds a pure joy because of the promise of ultimate blessing—eternal life.

However, there is another big idea that is a warning to all those who lack wisdom: A man who lacks godly wisdom is double-minded and unstable. A double-minded man will hedge his bets, asking God to intervene while, at the same moment, maintaining doubts. James follows up this statement with an example involving two men—one who is poor and the other who is rich. In this example, worldly values would put the rich man in an economically high position and the other man in a low position. However, James declares that in God's economy the one who is poor is in a high position because he knows that his only hope is in trusting God, and "the one who is rich … [is] in a low position," because he has hedged his bets on his wealth.

But James is not finished with his first exhortation. He points out another perspective that reveals double-mindedness and instability—blaming God for trials and temptations. This flawed perspective is a pathway to death! James 1:13–14 identifies a human tendency of shifting blame to a holy God for tempting me with hardship and struggles. "For God cannot be tempted by evil nor does he tempt anyone; but each one is tempted when by his own evil desire, he is dragged away and enticed" (James 1:13-14). This is a classic double-minded human argument that on one hand pretends to trust God for deliverance from trials while at the same time blaming God for allowing me to experience temptation through suffering.

Solomon graphically illustrates this truth in Proverbs 7:7–23 in his story about "a youth who lacked judgment" yielding to his own desires. He describes this double-minded young man flirting with temptation as he unwisely goes down the street toward a prostitute. Playing with his physical desires and ignoring what he knows is wrong, the youth allows the woman to embrace him, flatter him, and ultimately seduce him. The suffering that results from his flirting with danger directly relates to his "own evil desire" that "gives birth to sin" (James 1:15).

In contrast to Solomon's examples of a double-minded approach to a broken world, James concludes his first lesson on post-resurrection godly wisdom declaring that God's "good and perfect" (James 1:17) plan in the midst of a world "full of trials of many kinds" (James 1:2) is unwaveringly about choosing to give us a new "birth through the word of truth" (James 1:18). This is the same truth that Jesus declared to Nicodemus in his conversation about becoming "born again" in John 3. Nicodemus does not believe in the truth of Jesus' words because he is double-minded at that point in his faith journey. On the other hand, the Samaritan woman and the royal official in John 4 receive new life because they are single-minded in their belief. Both are examples of those who are in the high position of humble circumstances for saving grace, while Nicodemus is a perfect example of those who are in the low position of being rich in worldly religious traditions that have no power to save them.

SO WHAT?

Godly wisdom is available to those who have faith; however, faith is not faith if it is double-minded. The result of single-minded faith is the ability to have a joyful perspective on the trials and troubles of our broken world by viewing God's good and perfect eternal will through the lens of single-minded faith that produces mature perseverance by allowing us to see through the temporary to the eternal.

In His wisdom, God created a world that exhibits and requires the power of faith. Everyone practices faith to a greater or lesser degree. In all cases, though, faith only succeeds when it is single-minded.

For example, when my son played high school basketball, he worked hard on his skills, anticipating that he will be in high-pressure competitive situations. However, he hated working on foul shooting until he experienced game situations when he stood at the line and missed his free throws. So he learned the hard way to practice his free throw skills. Throughout the season, we talked about the importance of having faith that he can make his shots under pressure. Sure enough, in an end-of-the-season tournament at the end of the game with the game on the line, he found himself on the foul line shooting one on one with his team losing by one point. He made both shots! After the game, I asked him about his mindset when he felt the pressure of making those free throws. He told me that he wanted to be in that position because he knew he would make both shots. In other words, he had single-minded faith being sure of what he hoped for and certain of what he did not see yet. He didn't fix his eyes on doubt and nerves because he was sure of what he hoped for and certain of the outcome.

Along with James, writers of the New Testament in a post-resurrection world call believers to what can only be stated as godly wisdom that focuses on the unseen eternal promises that Jesus' death and resurrection pointed to. These promises were anticipated in Solomon's godly wisdom curriculum that warned that worldly values have an expiration date—death.

There are two powerful insights that James shares with his audience of Christian believers. Insight number 1 describes the power we experience when we have a wartime mindset of persevering through inevitable trials and troubles that come our way. There is nothing more effective for pointing to God's kingdom than single-mindedly focusing on an eternal perspective when in the midst of suffering. Nothing is more powerful for effectively modeling eternal values when we persevere with pure joy despite the trials and troubles of a sinful world. On the other hand, James shares a second powerful insight about when we fail to have an eternal perspective on evil and we double-mindedly blame God. Not all is lost if we focus on the truth that despite our failure to be single-minded, the greatest gift from above is the sacrificial death of Jesus our Lord, providing access to God's grace and forgiveness. James teaches us that when we consider it pure joy to faithfully persevere through the brokenness of a sinful world and when we humbly confess our own brokenness, we practice and exhibit life-saving godly wisdom.

James's godly wisdom first exhortation is about single-minded persevering faith that believes "every good and perfect gift is from above coming down from the Father of the heavenly heights who does not change like shifting shadows" (James 1:17). When we live out faith in Him, we are "blessed …

because when [we have] stood the test, [we] will receive the crown of life that God has promised to those who love Him" (James 1:12). Godly wisdom is single-mindedly eternally focused.

Faithful single-mindedness is focused on one truth and one truth only—despite trials, suffering, and troubles in our temporal world the eternal God has promised us that we will "dwell in the house of the LORD" (Ps. 23:6) When we know the destination, we can endure the journey, and even "consider it pure joy" when we encounter "trials of many kinds" on our way to eternity with our LORD.

CHAPTER 8 JAMES 1:1–18 STUDY GUIDE

1. **Read James 1:1–18**
- "A *servant* of God and the Lord Jesus Christ" How would you describe yourself if you had to start a general letter to an important group?

- First "my brothers" instruction
  - "Consider it pure joy …"
    - If you were to describe "pure joy," what would you say?

    - What is the reason for pure joy in verse 3?

  - The importance of developing perseverance
    - What do you think is the connection between perseverance and wisdom?

  - The importance of being single-minded
    - True belief is single-minded, not double-minded.
    - Belief after being tested requires …

- God's economy is the opposite of worldly economy.
  - Use Matthew 23:12 to explain this comment.

- What is the reward for persevering? (James 1:12)

- What are some of the consequences of not persevering?
  - See 1 John 1:5–10.

- Wisdom mindset description
  - What big idea about godly wisdom does this reiterate?

Application

According to James 1: 1–18, what does it look like to live out post-resurrection godly wisdom?

When have you been double-minded in your trust in God? What were you thinking?

When have you persevered through trouble or a trial single-mindedly trusting in God? What did you feel? What happened?

Why is it important to persevere through the inevitable trials and troubles of life?

9

TRUE LISTENING

James 1:19–27

"My brothers" exhortation #2: Post-resurrection godly wisdom is exhibited by listening to and acting on God's Word. (True listening always leads to doing.)

We had returned to New Jersey on home assignment after serving for four years at Rift Valley Academy in Kijabe, Kenya. Those years were the most thrilling and fulfilling years of our marriage. We had served as dorm parents for twenty-eight senior boys. I taught senior-year language arts and served as the English Department head. My wife, in addition to being a dorm mom to all those boys, served as a tutor and a keyboard instructor. Furthermore, I had been approached about the possibility of becoming the high school principal when we returned after our home assignment year.

During the ensuing year, we communicated with our supporters and felt their ongoing support for us to return to Rift Valley Academy. Our son was a freshman at the Air Force Academy, our oldest daughter had graduated from college and had begun a new job, and our middle daughter was in her last year of college. Everything seemed to be in order until my wife announced that she did not want to return to Kenya.

I was shocked! Just five years earlier, we had prayerfully made the decision for me to retire from my public-school teaching and coaching positions, and by faith raise support to become full-time missionaries. We were affirmed in every step. Our supporters and friends were enthusiastic about our decision. From the first day we arrived in Kenya, our work at Rift Valley Academy had been fulfilling, and, there was the prospect of possibly returning to a new position of influence. However, my wife simply and firmly stated she "wanted to remain in the States to be near our children."

Spontaneously, I cited all the compelling arguments against her wishes. She didn't change her mind. I escalated my efforts of persuasion by insisting that we ask our supporters what their impressions were of where we should be after our home assignment year. Even when the results of our survey showed a unanimous consensus that we should return to RVA, she didn't change her mind. I asked each of our three children to weigh in on our decision, and they confirmed that they saw us back in Kenya. She didn't change her mind!

I got angry and assailed her with predictions of incurring debts, losing our home, and being unemployed if we had to discontinue serving as African Inland Mission missionaries. I highlighted that I could not return to public school teaching because I had retired. Still, she insisted that she did not want to return to Kenya and RVA. I told her we had been called to this mission. I ranted about the new job I might have waiting for me—a job I had always dreamed about. Daily, we argued, until out of frustration, I would slam the door as I escaped to go on long walks. Finally, I played my trump card: She needed to submit to me because I was the head of the house! However, what I thought would produce checkmate produced a stalemate!

So I decided to talk to God about my rebellious and stubborn wife. While piously demanding that God change *her* and make *her* sensible, I felt a conviction to stop pleading and listen to God. As I went down on my knees, I felt the Spirit's prompting for me to consider my stubbornness, my ambitions, and my pride. In a posture of listening instead of demanding, I came to admit that *my* will was at the center of my demands. When I mentioned to God that he had called us to this mission, I recognized for the first time that His calling was to both of us, not just me. Then I remembered I was to love my wife as I love myself, and I knew what I had to do.

It was not easy! I went to my wife to confess my stubbornness, my ambition, my pride, and, most of all, my lack of empathy for her. Even in that confession, I tried to reason with her, saying, "I realize now that if I love you I need to submit to you just as I have insisted that you submit to me. *But*," I told her, with the hope it would change her mind, "this means we are going to enter into uncertain times if I can't find a job." When that did not make a difference, I yielded, and we agreed to trust that God would lead us to the next phase of our life together.

One month later, I was hired to be the principal of Eastern Christian Elementary School, which began a new, exciting, and fulfilling fifteen-year tenure at Eastern Christian School. As I entered into this new assignment, I felt God equipping me and recognized that our four years at RVA had prepared us for this new mission of serving the students and families of Eastern Christian School.

Proverbs 1:8–32 (First Listen) to James 1:19–27 (Be Quick to Listen)

In Proverbs 1:8, Solomon's first baseline instruction about godly wisdom begins with the word "listen." In this first instruction about godly wisdom, Solomon highlights the importance of listening, when Lady Wisdom warns that "the waywardness of the simple will kill them, and the complacency of fools will destroy them; but whoever listens to me will live in safety and be at ease, without fear of harm" (Prov. 1:32, 1:33). Nineteen times in his wisdom curriculum found in the first nine chapters of Proverbs, Solomon repeats the idea that listening *first* is an essential trait of godly wisdom for attaining discipline and direction.

Similarly, James emphasizes the importance of being "quick to listen."

> My dear brothers, take note of this: Everyone should be quick to listen, slow to speak, and slow to become angry, for man's anger does not bring about the righteous life that God desires. Therefore, get rid of all moral filth, and

> the evil that is so prevalent, and humbly accept the word planted in you, which can save you. (James 1:19–21)

James prescribes the act of *listening* as an antidote to anger and misunderstanding that leads to "moral filth and evil" (James 1:21). He is not merely saying that listening first is a good way to show empathy. He is saying that godly wisdom always maintains a listening posture and composure, exemplified by a humble confidence in God's word and promises. In fact, being quick to listen, slow to speak, and slow to become angry is a godly wisdom strategy that allows a pause to consider the "word planted in you" (James 1:21). This harkens back to the gospel of Mark, where Mark records two such parables, emphasizing the importance of listening. The parable of the sower begins with "Listen!" (Mark 4:3) and concludes with "He who has ears to hear, let him hear" (Mark 4:9). In Mark 4:13–20, he follows this parable with Jesus' explanation to his disciples, repeating the word "hear" four times. Then Mark quotes Jesus' parable about a lamp on a stand, closing that illustration with "If anyone has ears to hear, let him hear. Consider carefully what you hear" (Mark 4:23, 4:24).

Listening first allows me time to become aware of any selfish moral filth and evil that corrupts truth and blinds me from acting wisely. But James also warns that listening to the word is not enough, lest we think we can be passive in our faith. By bluntly stating, "Do what *it* says," (James 1:22), James declares that hearing it is not enough. Jesus warned, "Not everyone who says … 'Lord, Lord,' will enter the kingdom of heaven, but only he who *does* the will of my Father who is in heaven" (Matt. 7:27). The antecedent for the pronoun "*it*" of "Do what it says" (James 1:22) is "the perfect law that gives freedom" (James 1:25). James's fellow believers would know "the perfect law" is the moral Old Testament law of the Ten Commandments. However, it is also Jesus' new command to love one another as he has loved us. By succinctly declaring, "Do what it says," James is saying that listening is not hearing until we do what it says. The wisdom in this statement becomes clear when we follow the perfect law, as Jesus summarized it, freeing us from the prison of self-serving our temporary kingdom to serve his eternal kingdom by sacrificially loving others.

James concludes his second exhortation with a warning and two examples of what he means by doing what the perfect law says.

> If anyone considers himself religious and yet does not keep a tight rein on his tongue, he deceives himself and his religion is worthless. Religion that God our Father accepts as pure and faultless is this; to look after orphans and widows in their distress and to keep oneself from being polluted by the world. (James 1:26, 1:27)

By warning about hypocritical actions of just voicing our beliefs and intentions but never acting on them, James shows that the perfect law is not just about saying the right things about faith and belief. Then he points to two actions of what it looks like to not only listen to but also to do what the perfect law says: looking after orphans and widows and avoiding everything that is false in our world. By stating the specific example of looking after those in distress and stating the general example of avoiding the pollution of the world, James provides a wide spectrum of "doing what it says" actions that listening to God's word always leads to.

WHY IS THIS SO IMPORTANT?

To heed correction requires focused listening that leads to action. Heeding includes careful listening that leads to active responses. Heeding leads to prudence. Prudence leads to sound judgment, and sound judgment leads to wise actions. James points out that a person who foolishly rejects discipline is in danger of being deceived and lost. It is very much like looking into a mirror and seeing the need to take action on what is seen but refusing to do anything about it. A fool is offended by discipline. A wise person humbly accepts discipline that leads to taking action.

A person who is quick to speak and express anger does not have time for listening and learning. Perhaps you have a story like mine about being so convinced by ambition and ego that you refused to listen, choosing to be quick to speak and express anger. Ambition, ego, and self-centeredness have the ability to make us deaf and dumb. We are too busy listening to our own narrative about our own plans, and even when we are confronted with the convicting evidence that we are on a pathway toward evil and moral filth, we foolishly walk away and immediately forget.

When we read James and hear his stern warnings, we might lose sight of his positive emphasis on the result of living wisely in a broken post-resurrection world. James does not back away from pointing to the harsh consequences of unwise actions. Yet in every instruction, he cites the eternal benefits of godly wisdom. First, after identifying our world's brokenness that brings inevitable trials and troubles, he urges us to consider it pure joy to persevere because in the end, we grow "mature and complete ... lacking nothing" (James 1:4). Then James warns about temptations that threaten to drag us into desires that "gives birth to sin, and ... when it is full grown, gives birth to death" (James 1:15). But he follows this dire warning, reminding us that we can defeat temptations by remembering, "Every good and perfect gift is from above, coming down from the Father" (James 1:17). Thirdly, James condemns a common flaw of focusing on our own wisdom, refusing to listen while being quick to manipulate others with our words and anger to get what we want. However, he points out that we have access to [God's] "perfect law that gives freedom" (James 1:25).

SO WHAT?
(ADAM, EVE, AND ME)

When I choose to listen to my own self-centered internal narrative instead of God's word, I am continuing the legacy that began with Adam and Eve. They had only one law to follow, one rule to heed, one voice to trust. Yet they chose to listen to a lie that fit their desire to be autonomous. That decision led to being cast out of a perfect garden into a broken world and into a broken relationship with their Creator. Consequently, we all have inherited divided hearts that lean toward choosing our own designs and plans while rejecting God's good and perfect design. In Proverbs 1–9, Solomon illustrates this struggle between that which promises temporary pleasure and that which promises lasting value. By personifying worldly wisdom as Lady Folly, the Adulteress, and godly wisdom as Lady Wisdom, Solomon concludes his instruction in Proverbs 9 by describing how both women plan separate banquets and invite all those who hear to their parties. Invitees must decide which invitation to heed. Both invitations begin with the same words: "Let all who are simple come in here!" (Prov. 9:4, 9:16).

Lady Wisdom's invitation is transparent and direct: "Come and eat my food and drink the wine I have mixed. Leave your simple ways and you will live; walk in the way of understanding … the fear of the LORD is the beginning of wisdom, and the knowledge of the Holy One is understanding" (Prov. 9:5–6, 9:10). Her invitation includes full disclosure of a promise and a warning: "For through me your days will be many, and years will be added to your life. If you are wise your wisdom will reward you; if you are a mocker, you alone will suffer" (Prov. 9:11–12).

However, Lady Folly's invitation to those who lack judgment emphasizes salacious innuendo: "Stolen water is sweet: food eaten in secret is delicious" (Prov. 9:17). There is no such promise or warning from Lady Folly, but Solomon adds a chilling comment that concludes his entire instruction on godly wisdom: "But little do they [those who attend Lady Folly's party] know that the dead are there, that [her] guests are in the depths of the grave" (Prov. 9:18).

These two invitations could not be any more different. One invitation promises long life and wisdom. The other makes no promises but uses seductive hints knowing there are many who will opt for temporary pleasures that feed carnal desires over the eternal benefits of godly wisdom. Solomon's final pronouncement should evoke our need to be quick to listen to godly wisdom instead of other voices that lead to the grave. In other words, this is a life-or-death issue!

Frankly, I know I crave rebellion and the excitement of the moment. Thus, I am capable of rejecting Lady Wisdom's invitation in favor of going my own way. By valuing false promises of sensual delight and gratification, I can think, "What's the harm in having a little fun? I deserve it." Ironically,

Lady Wisdom's banquet also offers physical pleasures of well-prepared food and fine wine. Yet despite the promise of goodness and long life, as a rebel, I lean toward choosing friendship with the world rather than knowing and understanding the Holy One.

So what is the remedy for my deadly double-mindedness?

Simply stated, the remedy James teaches tells me is to listen to the word planted in me and act wisely by first believing in Jesus' sacrifice of taking my place on the cross so that I can receive eternal forgiveness and be free to love others.

John describes in his gospel (John 7:2–5) how Jesus' brothers saw him as a public figure, a politician who needed to become popular. They offered worldly advice about becoming a celebrity. So when Jesus submits to death on a criminal's cross, the disciples abandon him, confirming their unbelief. However, imagine what it must have been like for James and his brothers to experience Jesus' resurrection firsthand. Suddenly, all of Jesus' teachings began to make eternal sense. We have the benefit of reading eyewitness accounts of Jesus' resurrection informed by hindsight of his prophetic words. We have Jesus' Sermon on the Mount highlighting God's eternal kingdom values recorded in Matthew and Luke. We have the advantage of firsthand accounts about how He lived those values while extending an invitation for all to follow Him. We have firsthand descriptions and testimonies of Jesus submitting to the cross and receiving God's punishment for the sins of the world. And we have eyewitness accounts of Jesus' resurrection and ascension into heaven.

In Jesus' conversation with Nicodemus, recorded in John 3, Jesus alluded to Numbers 21:8 and 21:9 and the story of Moses raising an image of a snake in the wilderness.

> I have spoken to you of earthly things and you do not believe; how then will you believe if I speak of heavenly things? Just as Moses lifted up the snake in the desert, so the Son of Man must be lifted up. That everyone who believes in him may have eternal life. (John 3:12, 3:14–15)

Nicodemus would later understand what Jesus meant by this allusion when he witnessed Jesus lifted up and nailed to a cross. So at the end of John's Gospel, John reports that Nicodemus joined Joseph of Arimathea in requesting Jesus' body to bury it in a tomb. Nicodemus "brought a mixture of myrrh and aloes, about seventy-five pounds" (John 19:39). This decision to honor Jesus' sacrifice on the cross and risk his reputation as a Pharisee, along with Joseph of Arimathea is an act, not just words, of faith.

How much more so, from where we stand in our post-resurrection world, do we have the advantage of hindsight to see the completed story of Jesus' redemptive death on a cross, and just as the wandering Israelites were saved by the simple act of faith, wherein by looking at the image they would be cured, we are rescued from the threat of eternal death by looking to Jesus. Looking is an act of believing. When we recognize that we cannot be our own savior and we look to the empty cross knowing that Jesus died for our warped hearts, we are saved. In our new birth as children of God, we are transformed and free to live wisely as children of God aware that every good and perfect gift comes from our Father in heaven.

Yet knowing that children of God need godly wisdom instruction, James writes to his brother believers, instructing them about what it looks like to live wisely in a post-resurrection world that threatens to push them in the wrong direction away from God. His warnings about living intentionally for God's kingdom values are an extension of Solomon's warnings about staying on the pathway of wisdom by trusting in the Lord with all your heart and acknowledging him in all your ways (Prov. 3:5, 3:6). Because we are redeemed does not guarantee us from being polluted by this world by forgetting whom we serve. That is why we need to daily "fix our eyes on Jesus, the author and perfecter of our faith" (Heb. 12:2).

My story about being influenced by my ego and ambition illustrates how it is possible, even with good intentions, to drift away from God's will and instead follow my corrupt will, leaning on my own understanding instead of listening to God's will. Daily listening first to God's word and doing what it says by fixing my eyes on Jesus is the remedy for double-minded deception.

~ Richard Van Yperen ~

Now in our fiftieth year of marriage, my wife smiles whenever I share our story about my having to submit to her and God. Every time I retell the story of my self-centered ambition, I include the following sentence: "I had to stutter the three toughest words for a husband to declare—'I was wr-wro-wrong!'" But great rewards were realized: a stronger marriage, a growing understanding of God's will, forgiveness, and a humble desire to serve others.

CHAPTER 9 JAMES 1:19–27 STUDY GUIDE

1. **Review James 1:1–18**
   - *What* do we need to know as believers living in a post-resurrection world?
     - Attitude: "Consider it pure joy"
     - Disposition: Perseverance
     - Mindset: Single-mindedness
     - Inclination: Humility
   - *Why* do we need to apply the above *what*s?

   - *So what* is the result?
     - James 1:12

     - James 1:18

2. **Read Ephesians 6:10–18.**
   - Why does Paul give these instructions?

3. **Review James 1:19–27, "My brothers" exhortation #2.**
   - *What* do we need to know?

   - "Everyone should be
     - quick to _____,
     - slow to _____
     - and slow to _____.,
     - for man's _____
     - does not _____."

- "Therefore,
  - get rid of *all* _____ …
  - and humbly accept _____."
- *Why* do we need these instructions" (Hint: Think about Paul's instructions in Ephesians.)

- Wisdom's posture and disposition
  - What does it look like to follow this instruction?

  - What does it feel like to follow this instruction?

- (James 1:22) "*Do not* merely listen to the word, _____"

- "*Do* what it says!"
  - What is the antecedent for the pronoun "it"?

- (James1:23–27) Two practical examples of doing what it says:
  - Example 1:

    - Application: Blessing is the result and fruit of hearing and acting on God's words.

  - Example 2:

- Application: Being religious is about controlling the tongue and caring about others.

4. *So what* fears, doubts, anxieties, and thoughts prevent you from heeding God's word and doing what it says? Make a list below.

WISDOM REJECTS FAVORITISM

James 2:1–13

"My brothers" exhortation #3: Post-resurrection wisdom rejects favoritism.

In his third "My brothers" instruction about living out godly wisdom in a post-resurrection world, James exposes the subtle hypocrisy of prejudicial favoritism.

> Suppose a man comes into your meeting wearing a gold ring and fine clothes, and a poor man in shabby clothes also comes in. If you show special attention to the man wearing fine clothes and say, Here's a good seat for you, but say to the poor man, "You stand there" or "Sit on the floor by my feet," have you not discriminated among yourselves and become judges with evil thoughts? (James 2:2–4)

In this scenario, James is not saying it is wrong to give a good seat to a rich person. There is nothing wrong with providing a seat for a guest. However, the wrong James is pointing to is the special attention given to one person because he appears to have wealth while at the same time deliberately not providing a seat for a poor man. This kind of overt discrimination reflects motivations that James identifies as "evil thoughts" (James 2:4).

At first glance, this instruction may seem minor. However, evil thoughts of favoritism create discrimination that furthers a worldly order of inequality in which people compete for power, influence, superiority, and advantage. James gives three kingdom principles for how to live out post-resurrection godly wisdom that rejects hypocritical favoritism.

1. God has "chosen those who are poor in the eyes of the world to be rich in faith and to inherit the kingdom he promised those who love him" (James 2:5).

James uses a list of four rhetorical questions to reveal the truth about favoritism (James 2:5–8):

- Has not God chosen those who are poor in the eyes of the world to be rich in faith and to inherit the kingdom he promised those who love him?
- Is it not the rich who are exploiting you?
- Are they [rich people] not the ones who are dragging you into court?
- Are they [rich people] not the ones who are slandering the noble name to whom you belong?

Because God sent Jesus to rescue the lost, oppressed, poor, prisoners, and those who are blind, his followers are not to show favoritism for the wealthy at the expense of those who are poor. When we solely favor those who are wealthy, we reveal self-serving motivations that seek favor from sources other than God. By doing so, James says we join those who insult and slander the "noble name of Him to whom [we] belong" (James 2:7), the same people who will oppose and exercise power over us when it is convenient for them.

2. Through Moses, David, and Jesus, God has established the royal law—"Love your neighbor as yourself" (James 2:8).

James points to the royal law as the primary law that encompasses the entire law. If we break that law, we become guilty of breaking the entire law. Loving my neighbor includes not only all believers but all people. Worldly culture breaks the royal law by practicing prejudice, favoritism, and discrimination that divides people into rankings. This is not love! James puts breaking the royal law on the same level as committing murder (James 2:11).

3. God has shown that "mercy triumphs over judgment" (James 2:13).

Finally, and most powerfully, James identifies mercy as a kingdom value that "triumphs over judgment." Judgment is a fearful thing for all of Adam and Eve's descendants who fall short of the law (all humans!). However, Jesus came to make mercy triumph over judgment through his substitutionary death. By paying the ultimate price for our sins, Jesus frees us to receive God's mercy instead of his judgment. On the other hand, if we have received mercy instead of judgment but we then exercise judgment over others instead of mercy, we are like the unmerciful servant in Jesus' parable who received mercy and forgiveness from a king but refused to extend mercy to a fellow servant (Matt. 18: 23–35). When the master found out about what his servant had done, he "turned him over to the jailers to be tortured, until he should pay back all he owed." Jesus then declares, "This is how my Heavenly Father will treat each of you."

Why is this so important?

James is calling out any believer who shows favoritism. But isn't this just a banal fact of our world? Showing favoritism is so common in all areas of society that one might think that James is using hyperbole when he labels it evil. Certainly, favoritism is unfair, but is it really evil? What makes an action evil? By labeling it "evil *thoughts*" (James 2:4), James points out that evil actions originate with an internal mindset. The result of "evil thoughts" leads to natural self-serving motivations that further personal kingdom values rather than God's kingdom values. In other words, evil is anything that seeks to thwart God's kingdom values in favor of one's personal advancement.

In fact, evil entered all creation through the evil of a kind of favoritism. Adam and Eve chose to favor their own ends and desires over God's authority by seeking worldly wisdom and knowledge of good and evil. In other words, they rejected God's lordship in favor of self-rule. This choice set the pattern of sinful behavior for all of Adam and Eve's descendants.

The result is a world full of self-serving favoritism that strives to gain an advantage over others. When we open our eyes to this truth, we begin to understand why Jesus, the second Adam, came to redress the wrongs of a world that rejects eternal values in favor of gaining temporary power and influence. Jesus came to model eternal values and "call sinners to repentance" (Luke 5:32). He intentionally moved away from the religious elite and toward those who are poor in spirit and not favored, like the Samaritan woman who had had five husbands, tax collectors like Matthew and Zacchaeus, and many who were ostracized because of illness and disease. His parables about the lost sheep, the lost coin, and a lost son rebuked the favoritism of the Pharisees and affirmed the value of the poor, the lost, and those who are marginalized. His beatitudes at the beginning of the Sermon on the Mount declared those who are poor in spirit, who mourn, who are meek, and who hunger are blessed because great is their reward in eternity.

SO WHAT?

Favoritism breaks the law! We know this to be true, not only because James says it. We know it in our hearts. Ironically, when I practice favoritism, I reason that it is not that bad because everyone does it; but when I experience favoritism's unfair betrayal and rejection, I am quick to call it evil.

In anticipation of his imminent death, Jesus gives his disciples a new command, "Love one another, as I have loved you, so you must love one another. By this all men will know that you are my disciples, if you love one another" (John 13:34, 13:35). Like the royal law, this new command sums up the entire law. Jesus had modeled mercy, grace, and love for his disciples, but not just for his cohort of twelve followers. After stating this new command, Jesus deliberately emphasizes that his love is available to *anyone*. "If *anyone* loves me, he will obey my teaching. My Father will love him and we will come to him and make our home with him" (John

14:23). Similarly, earlier in his nighttime conversation with Nicodemus, Jesus states that he will be lifted up so that "*everyone* who believes in him may have eternal life. For God so loved the [*everyone* in the] world [not just the disciples.] that He gave His only begotten son that *whoever* believes in Him shall not perish but have eternal life" (John 3:14b–16). We can easily miss the order in these famous verses. God first "loved the world," so then "He gave His one and only son, so "that *whoever* believes' will receive eternal life" (John 3:14–16). (Note my emphasis on the inclusive pronouns.) Whoever includes all levels of society.

Because favoritism naturally lurks in my heart's desires, it subtly influences my attitudes, thoughts, and words long before it is revealed by my actions. Motivated by my desire for recognition and power, I put myself on the throne of my life and demand the right to discriminate between winners and losers. Motivated by self-lordship, my favoritism mindset forms mental judgments with the purpose of labeling and ranking them. I do this by observing people in public, in church, and in relationships. In my judgments, I edify my self-worth by denigrating others' worth. Because this behavior is internal and subtle, I don't realize these thoughts are evil. If not confronted, my judging and labeling will lead to secret prejudicial attitudes, which, if left unchecked, will result in hurtful discriminatory actions.

James's exhortation confronts this worldly mindset of favoritism as an evil that is the height of hypocrisy for those who have received mercy instead of judgment through Jesus' sacrificial death. To not extend the same mercy to others undermines everything Jesus taught.

CHAPTER 10 JAMES 2:1–13 STUDY GUIDE

Review James 2:1–13 "My brothers" exhortation #3.

- *What* do we need to know?
  - What are the three kingdom principles about favoritism in this passage?

- *Why* is this godly wisdom?

- *So what* difference does this instruction make?

- **Application**
  - Have you ever been accused of favoritism?
  - Where do you see subtle favoritism in your neighborhood, work, circles of influence, politics, and government?
  - How can you extend mercy in the context of the above areas?

11

FAITH AND ACTIONS

James 2:14–3:18

"My brothers" exhortation #4: Post-resurrection wisdom will always be verified through faith and actions working together (James 2:14–26).

So far, in his letter to his Christian brothers, James instructs them

- to be single-minded in their faith by getting "rid of all moral filth and evil" and accepting "the word planted in [them]" (James 1:21),
- to show "pure and faultless religion" (James 1:27) not just by what one says but also by what one does to serve others, and
- to reject favoritism by loving others as yourself.

Each of these instructions seeks to affirm that godly wisdom will always result in actions that reflect eternal values. Godly wisdom is not esoteric; it is validated by kingdom-focused actions that reveal eternal values.

This idea is further developed in the next instruction, James 2:14–26. Once again, James uses rhetorical questions.

> Question #1: What good is it, my brothers, if a man claims to have faith but has no deeds? (James 2:14)
> The implied answer is this: If faith is not evidenced by good deeds, faith is false.

> Question #2: Suppose a brother or sister is without clothes and food. If one of you says to him, "Go, I wish you well; keep warm and well fed," but does nothing about his physical needs, what good is it? (James 2:15, 2:16)

The implied answer is a loud "It is not good at all!" In fact, it is cynical.

> Question #3: But someone will say, "You have faith; I have deeds." You foolish man, do you want evidence that faith without deeds is useless? (James 2:18, 2:20)

James offers his answer by asking another rhetorical question about how Abraham's act of faith in God "was made complete by what he did. Was not our ancestor Abraham considered righteous for what he did when he offered his son Isaac on the altar?" (James 2:21).

The implied answer is an even louder "drop the mic" affirmation emphatically stating, "You see that a person is justified by what he does not by faith alone" (James 2:24).

Why is this important?

"Even the demons believe" in God (James 2:19). However, that kind of belief is reluctant intellectual recognition that God exists. Demons believe that there is one God because they have had firsthand experience in having been expelled from heaven by God. This kind of belief is inconsequent because it is merely knowledge.

To emphasize his point about faith and deeds, James concludes this instruction with a shockingly remarkable example. Out of all the life examples in the famous faith heroes chapter, Hebrews 11, James chooses the historical story of Rahab, a Gentile prostitute, who acted on her belief that the spies she hid were servants of the true God.

> Was not even Rahab the prostitute considered righteous for what she did when she gave lodging to the spies and sent them off in a different direction? As the body without

the spirit is dead, so faith without deeds is dead. (James 2:25, 2:26)

Her story is told in Joshua 22. She is included in the Hall of Faith chapter, and James uses her example as surprising proof of the power of faith-filled deeds. Finally, James's Christian brothers would have known that Matthew identified this former prostitute as an ancestor of Jesus (see Matt. 1:5). Because of a simple act of faith that had huge implications—the eventual birth of the Messiah—a Gentile prostitute is mentioned four times in scripture!

SO WHAT?

If my deeds are the outcomes of my beliefs and those outcomes become my life legacy, sadly, my legacy is only about exclusively striving for the temporary values of this world, and I have missed my calling to serve as a child of God. However, like Rahab the prostitute, or even the Samaritan woman at the well, God pursues us despite our past actions, calling us to transformational faith in him that influences others for eternity. In the context of biblical history recorded for all time, Rahab's belief led to hiding the spies who saved an entire nation and a Samaritan woman's newfound faith resulted in evangelizing an entire town. In both examples, God worked through the faith of the least for the good of his eternal kingdom, and lives were saved.

Biblical scholars have written that James's letter to his fellow brothers in Christ was one of the earliest of New Testament writings. Likely, his instructions about authentic faithful living were absolutely essential if Christianity was going to grow. James knew that "believers" who declared their faith publicly but failed to follow through on what they said would be perceived as hypocrites, and the message of the gospel would then suffer.

Historians have confirmed that Christianity changed the world because of the legacy of faithful believers. So what will historians write about contemporary Christian believers one hundred years from now? James's instruction remains relevant two thousand plus years later. Worldly voices encouraging me to follow my heart, define my identity, pursue wealth, gratify my desires, and strive for autonomy are ubiquitous and compelling. Like Solomon's instructive proverbs about godly wisdom, James provides New Testament instruction about what it takes to faithfully pursue godly wisdom in a post-resurrection world. Additionally, like Solomon, James balances his precepts with exhortations warning against unwise worldly living, emphasizing that self-serving and hypocritical actions lead to the grave. "As the body without the spirit is dead, so faith without deeds is dead" (James 2:26).

So let's review what James has instructed and warned, so far, about being a believer in a post-resurrection world.

1. *Instructed:* True belief will persevere single-mindedly, despite trials and trouble. *Warned:* A double-minded person will be "unstable in all he does" (James 1:8).
2. *Instructed:* True belief will exhibit humility by listening to the word of God and getting rid of all moral filth and evil. *Warned:* "Anyone who listens to the word but does not do what it says … deceives himself" (James 1:23).
3. *Instructed:* True belief will emphasize favor and reject favoritism. Mercy trumps judgment. *Warned:* Anyone who does not "love his neighbor as himself" is guilty of breaking the entire law (James 2:8).
4. *Instructed:* True belief will affect others through actions that verify belief. *Warned:* Faith by itself, if it is not accompanied by action, is dead (James 2:17).

James is not creating a new law that must be followed. These precepts are not about being good enough to enter heaven. No one is good enough!

> For all have sinned and fall short of the glory of God, and are justified by his grace as a gift, through the redemption that is in Christ Jesus, whom God put forward as a propitiation by his blood, to be received by faith. This was to show God's righteousness, because in his divine

forbearance he had passed over former sins (Rom. 3:23–25, ESV).

However, James's precepts are about the supernatural attributes of those who have "received by faith" the gift of "redemption that is in Christ Jesus" (Rom. 3:23–25, ESV). These kingdom attributes are the outgrowth of God's transforming work in his believers for the purpose of showing God's righteousness and grace.

James' teaching about true faith that is affirmed by deeds and false faith without deeds alludes to Jesus' teaching about who are the sheep and who are the goats in Matthew 25.

> Then the King will say to those [sheep] on his right, "Come, you who are blessed by my Father; take your inheritance, the kingdom prepared for you since the creation of the world. For I was hungry and you gave me something to eat, I was thirsty and you gave me something to drink, I was a stranger and you invited me in, I needed clothes and you clothed me, I was sick and you looked after me, I was in prison and you came to visit me." ... Then he will say to those [goats] on his left, "Depart from me, you who are cursed, into the eternal fire prepared for the devil and his angels. For I was hungry and you gave me nothing to eat, I was thirsty and you gave me nothing to drink, I was a stranger and you did not invite me in, I needed clothes and you did not clothe me, I was sick and in prison and you did not look after me." (Matt. 25:34–36, 25:41–43)

Compare this teaching by Jesus with James's example in James 2:14, 12:5–16.

> What good is it, my brothers if a man claims to have faith but has no deeds? Suppose a brother or sister is without clothes and daily food. If one of you says to him, "Go, I wish you well; keep warm and well fed," but does nothing about his physical needs, what good is it?

It is important to remember that James is writing to his brother believers scattered among the nations. His teaching is for the sheep, not the goats. Christ followers and believers—sheep—need James' practical instruction lest they step off the pathway of godly wisdom and begin to be influenced by worldly pursuits that lead them away from their calling to serve the Shepherd King of the eternal kingdom. James' wise exhortations and warnings are as relevant now for us, the Shepherd King's sheep who believe that he is the way, the truth, and the life (John 14:9). James knows that sheep are naive and easily led. So as sheep, we need to be reminded to listen to and then do what the Shepherd says because "anyone who listens to the word but does not do what it says" is like looking in a mirror and instead of acting on what is seen, immediately forgets what he looks like (James 1:23, 1:24). Faith without deeds is like taking time to read scripture but then forgetting what I have seen in the mirror of God's word. Too often, I spend time in God's word and then immediately enter into the fray of the day, forgetting what I read.

James digs deeper into his idea about faithful outcomes by writing about taming the tongue in James 3:1–18. He points to heroes of the faith at the end of chapter 2; then he provides this practical example of how words (the tongue) powerfully influence outcomes in the first part of chapter 3.

After reminding his brothers in Christ that "we all stumble in many ways" (James 3:2), James points out that a person who is "never at fault in what he says … is a perfect man able to keep his whole body in check" (James 3:2). By lamenting that such a small instrument [the tongue] is "a world of evil among parts of the body," he points out how impossible it is to control one's tongue (James 3:5). This irony—describing a perfect man who is never at fault in what he says but then proving that perfection is impossible because of a small part of the body—is affirmed with a blunt assertion:

> All kinds of animals, birds, reptiles and creatures of the sea are being tamed and have been tamed by man, but no man can tame the tongue. It is a restless evil, full of deadly poison. (James 3:7, 3:8)

Followed by a rebuke:

> With the tongue we praise our Lord and Father, and with it we curse men, who have been made in God's likeness. Out of the same mouth come praise and cursing. My brothers, this should not be. (James 3:9, 3:10)

(By the way, throughout this argument, James includes himself, using the pronoun "we.")

Finally, he uses rhetorical questions once again to drive home his point.

> Can both fresh water and salt water flow from the same spring? My brothers, can a fig tree bear olives, or a grapevine bear figs? Neither can a salt spring produce fresh water. (James 3:11)

James is echoing what Jesus taught when he was confronted by the Pharisees. "It is only by Beelzebub the prince of demons, that this fellow drives out demons" (Matt. 12:24). In his response to the Pharisees, Jesus includes his rebuke of their reasoning by saying,

> Make a tree good and its fruit will be good, or make a tree bad and its fruit will be bad, for a tree is recognized by its fruit. You brood of vipers how can you who are evil say anything good? For out of the overflow of the heart the mouth speaks. The good man brings good things out of the good stored up in him, and the evil man brings evil things out of the evil stored up in him." (Matt. 12:33–35)

Accordingly, James declares that true faith will produce consistent outcomes, but also according to James, we cannot produce faith-filled outcomes with our tongue because out of the overflow of our hearts, our words betray us. How am I to solve this conundrum about not being able to control my tongue and my heart? The answer to this question comes in the next six verses—James's fifth exhortation.

"My brothers" exhortation #5: Post-resurrection wisdom is pure, peace-loving, considerate, submissive, impartial, and sincere (James 3:13–18).

James writes about two types of wisdom—worldly wisdom that harbors "bitter envy and selfish ambition in your hearts," and heavenly wisdom that is first "pure, then peace-loving, considerate, submissive, full of mercy and good fruit, impartial and sincere" (James 3:14, 3:17). He states that the first wisdom comes from the devil and produces "disorder and every evil practice" (James 3:16), but the second wisdom comes from heaven and produces peace and "a harvest of righteousness" (James 3:18). The contrast is intentionally stark, and almost too much to accept because we are naturally double-minded, wanting to move back and forth between the two pearls of wisdom. When we want to advance our goals for personal success, we choose worldly wisdom. On the other hand, when we seek our soul yearning for purity, peace, and mercy, we choose godly wisdom. For many, the first choice is a weekday decision, and the second is a Sunday decision because we live in two worlds serving two masters—our ambitions and our God.

Why is this important?

James is again asserting that double-mindedness will produce fickle faith that ultimately serves one's immediate motivations, desires, and dreams. Fickle faith is able to exhibit momentary control over the tongue to serve a desire for recognition or for gaining power over others. Double-mindedness wants to be spiritual and worldly as the occasion dictates. But this is not biblical faith! It is a worldly attempt to masquerade my true intention to manipulate outcomes to serve myself. It is earthly wisdom that seeks earthly rewards. Single-minded faith serves only eternal kingdom values. It comes from outside, not from within. It is always humble, pure, peace-loving, considerate, submissive, and full of mercy.

Sam Allberry, in his book *James for You*, answers the obvious question, How is heavenly wisdom to be gained?

> There are two kinds of wisdom, and they are widely different. One comes from heaven, the other is earthly. One is spiritual; the other is unspiritual. One is from God, the other is from the devil (v.15). True wisdom, in other words, comes from outside this world. It comes from God alone, as the Proverb reminds us: "For the LORD gives wisdom; from his mouth come knowledge and understanding" (Prov. 2:6) And, as James has already told us: "If any of you lacks wisdom, you should ask God" (James 1:5). We cannot gain true wisdom without turning to God for it. If the source of wisdom is God we need to be those who pray. The fact is we need to have God's perspective on our lives. We need to humble our hearts. We need to tame our tongues. It is why humility and wisdom go together in this passage; to truly know yourself is to know yourself as someone in need of God's grace. (p. 101)

SO WHAT?

No level of effort or resolution will succeed in taming my tongue. I already know this by trying and failing. I know I need cleansing from the inside out. While I am naturally able to outwardly put on and put off behaviors that suit the occasion, I know that heart change requires a supernatural inner transformation that comes from above. Progressive change begins with a single-minded upward request for godly wisdom. In his book *Inside Out* (NavPress, Colorado Springs, Colorado, 1988), Dr. Larry Crabb describes how inner change is a growth process that begins with a conscious desire for permanent change.

> We move from *change in our conscious direction to change in our approach to relationships* to *change in the direction of our very being*. Each change represents a work of God and is therefore good. To label the first kind of change shallow would wrongly demean it. But to stop, with the first kind of change, or the second, reflects a failure to

> understand the opportunity we have to pursue God and to know Him. New believers change in their conscious direction. Growing believers learn to love by abandoning their self-protection. Mature believers begin to grasp the meaning of Paul's words, "For to me, to live is Christ," as they shift the central direction of their very being toward God. (pp. 202–203)

Growth does not happen in a vacuum. While it is not the main theme, Jesus' parable of the sower (Matt. 13:3–23) illustrates the importance of the soil in which faith grows. What soil is my/your faith planted in? The fruit of inner change and spiritual transformation will grow and ripen only if I tend to the soil by inviting the Holy Spirit to soften my heart, remove the rocks of doubt and pull the weeds of distractions, while I intentionally spend daily time in God's word fertilizing and watering my faith. However, faith will not grow if I keep pulling the plant up by its roots and replanting it as it serves my selfish whims, wishes, and schemes. That is double-minded gardening, and it will stunt spiritual faith.

So James focuses on contrasting aspects of two kinds of wisdom - the fruit of mature godly wisdom that produces "a harvest of righteousness" (James 3:18) and worldly wisdom that produces an unproductive life of ambitious efforts that are of the devil. Godly wisdom is evidenced by "deeds done in the humility that comes from wisdom" (James 3:13). Earthly wisdom harbors "bitter envy and selfish ambition" that leads to "disorder and every evil practice" (James 3:14, 3:16).

James identifies the qualities of godly wisdom as good fruit—"pure ... peace-loving, considerate, submissive, full of mercy ... impartial and sincere" (James 3:17). In another letter to believers, the apostle Paul provides a list of the qualities of [good] fruit of the Spirit: "love, joy, peace, patience, kindness, goodness, faithfulness, gentleness and self-control" (Gal. 5:22). Both authors intend their lists to serve an instructional purpose for evaluation and measurement. Each fruit attribute provides a growth marker of the Spirit's work in producing the good fruit of mature godly wisdom. With the Holy Spirit as my guide, each list allows me to evaluate where I need to "shift the central direction of [my] very being toward God." Solomon writes in his wisdom curriculum, "The fear of the LORD is the beginning of wisdom, and the knowledge of the Holy One is understanding" (Prov. 9:10). Godly wisdom orients my very being toward understanding the Holy One. That understanding is completed by Christ's death and resurrection, which demands my all in all.

Christ's death and resurrection settle my need to measure myself according to the law. Because I am forgiven for my past, present, and future sins, and I am accepted as a child of God, I am free to live by faith no longer for personal gain but for the sake of my Savior. This is what James is teaching his brothers in Christ—their good deeds are the natural products of faith that are anchored in good works designed to glorify the Father.

CHAPTER 11 JAMES 2:14–3:18 STUDY GUIDE

1. **Review James 2:14–26.**
   - Two essential questions about "faith" and "deeds." What do the two questions address?
     1.

     2.

   - Example and application
     a. Example:

     b. Application:

   - Argument about true faith
     o Note the word "believe" (James 2:19, 2:23). How does belief apply to the three examples below?
       - Demons

       - Abraham

       - Rahab

   - Explain James' comparison of Abraham and Rahab.

2. **Review James 3:1–12.**
   - How does this next instruction about the tongue connect with the instructions on faith and deeds?

3. **Review James 3:13–18, two kinds of wisdom.**
   - What are the two kinds of wisdom?
   1.

   2.

   - What is the connection between verse 17 and verse 18?

Application
"My brothers" exhortation #4: Post-resurrection godly wisdom will always be verified through faith and actions working together.

- If you were to evaluate a typical day of your life, what percentage of the day would you say your deeds point to your faith in God, and what percentage would point to your own agenda?

"My brothers" exhortation #5: Post-resurrection godly wisdom is pure, peace-loving, considerate, submissive, merciful, impartial, and sincere.

- These attributes "raise a harvest of righteousness" (James 3:18). What do you think that means? How do you think that works?

12

NOW LISTEN

James 4:1–5:6

Before we look at James's sixth "my brothers" exhortation in James 4:1–5:6, let's look at his emphasis so far. Just as Solomon had taught wisdom precepts in Proverbs by pointing out what to do as well as what not to do, so James teaches post-resurrection wisdom precepts. Through his precepts, James instructs his brother believers who are "scattered among the nations" (James 1:1) what they should do and what they are not to do.

- Knowing that "every good and perfect gift is from the Father who does not change" (James 1:17), believers are to persevere single-mindedly, and not be double-minded.
- Believers are to "be quick to listen, slow to speak and slow to become angry" (James 1:19), but "do not merely listen to the word … do what it says" (James 1:22).
- Believers are to serve others by loving their neighbor as they love themselves (James 2:8), and not show favoritism because "mercy triumphs over judgment" (James 2:13).
- Believers are to act on their faith, because "faith by itself, if it is not accompanied by action, is dead" (James 2:17).
- Believers are to choose godly wisdom that exhibits "deeds done in humility" (James 3:13), not "harbor bitter envy and selfish ambition" that produces "disorder and every evil practice" (James 3:14, 3:16).

"My brothers" exhortation #6: Post-resurrection wisdom exhibits submission to God evidenced by extending mercy and peace to others while rejecting envy and selfish ambition.

At the end of chapter 3, James appears to conclude his wisdom instruction by defining earthly wisdom and heavenly wisdom. After declaring that earthly wisdom originates in envy and selfish ambition, he writes two sentences that seem perfect for concluding his letter:

> But the wisdom that comes from heaven is first of all pure; then peace-loving, considerate, submissive, full of mercy, and good fruit, impartial and sincere. Peacemakers who sow in peace raise a harvest of righteousness. (James 3:17–18)

Seemingly, the only thing lacking is a football coach's challenge: "Now go out there and do it!"

But, without a transition, James shifts from his elevated idea about the fruit of godly wisdom to two blunt questions:

> What causes fights and quarrels among you? Don't they come from your desires that battle within you? (James 4:1)

James's rhetorical questions expose an inner reality that needs to be addressed. It has to do with the condition of one's heart. He has addressed the *what* and *why* of godly wisdom, but he knows that he still needs to address the question: *So what* do I need to do to be a peacemaker?

James follows his curt questions with accusatory language:

> You want something but don't get it. You kill and covet, but you cannot have what you want. You quarrel and fight. You do not have, because you do not ask God. When you ask, you do not receive, because you ask with wrong motives, that you may spend what you get on your pleasures. (James 4:2–3)

Once again, in his instruction, James returns to his motif of the absolute importance of single-minded faith by showing how selfish motives undermine not only our relationship with others but, more importantly, our relationship with God. James uses uncompromising language here to show how serious this is. A believer cannot be a peacemaker that sows a harvest of righteousness if he/she harbors wrong motives that produce quarrels and fights.

But James is not done accusing his brothers:

> You adulterous people don't you know that friendship with the world is hatred toward God? Anyone who chooses to be a friend of the world becomes an enemy of God. (James 4:4)

Adulterous? What is behind this offensive label? Adultery is committed when a person is unfaithful in a relationship. In this context, James is calling believers adulterous if they choose the values of the world over godly values.

James calls "friendship with the world" adulterous because it "is hatred toward God" (James 4:4). When asked what was the greatest commandment, Jesus had highlighted that the greatest commandment is "Love the Lord your God with all your heart and with all your soul, and with all your mind" (Matt. 22:37). It is that little word "all" that makes the difference. "All" leaves no room for exceptions. When he asks the followers, "What good is it for a man to gain the *whole* world yet forfeit his soul?" (Matt. 8:46), "whole" has the same meaning as "all." Choosing to favor the "whole world" leaves no room for loving God in "all" your ways. Therefore, we break the commandment if we make room for loving the world in our heart, our soul, and/or our mind. Here is James's big idea again about double-mindedness, but with an added charge—it is adulterous.

So what am I to do? James admonishes that my single-minded relationship with God requires that I submit, resist, come near, purify my heart, grieve, mourn, and humble myself. These are acts and attitudes of repentance and submission.

Before considering the importance of repentance, it might help for you to personalize James's question, "What causes fights and quarrels in your life?" (James 4:1). Think back to a conflict you had with your wife, your best friend, a colleague, or a fellow believer in the past. What happened? Why did it happen? Who was at fault?

I remember a conflict I had with a great friend who was willing to confront me about inappropriate behavior and a prideful attitude. I reacted to his intervention with anger and gave him the silent treatment for weeks. During that time, I convinced myself that he had no right to confront me. I thought, maybe if he were a little more empathetic I might consider what he had to say. I convinced myself that our conflict was his fault. However, I did not want him to expose my double-minded heart condition, so I resented his words and chose to reject him even at the risk of killing our friendship.

James knows that pride and selfish ambition distort perspective so that selfish desires when confronted will try to shift blame to avoid a humble reconciliation. "You want something but don't get it. You kill and covet, but you cannot have what you want" (James 4:2). The three words "I am wrong" are very difficult, if not impossible, to say when a prideful heart is in control. The very act of refusing to see the wrong in oneself betrays a willingness to kill a relationship rather than admit fault. Likewise, when James refers to wrong motives and evil desires that battle within you, he is saying the fault is yours because you are being faithful to those desires at the cost of being unfaithful to your relationship with God.

So James provides ten commands that address the need to root out the wrong motives of the heart. Pastor Tim Keller teaches that the Hebrew word for "heart" in the Bible includes the mind, will, and emotion. My "heart" is revealed when my mind ignores my convictions, when my will focuses on selfish desires, and when my emotions lose self-control. The results are dissension, quarrels, and fights, not peace.

Having labeled his brother believers, as well as his readers, adulterous, he prescribes the following commands in James 4:7–11:

- Submit yourselves, then, to God.
- Resist the devil, and he will flee from you.
- Come near to God and he will come near to you.
- Wash your hands, you sinners.
- Purify your hearts you double-minded.
- Grieve.
- Mourn.
- Wail.
- Humble yourselves before the Lord, and he will lift you up.
- Do not slander one another.

Having provided the evidence designed to convict his brother believers, he then provides corrective acts and attitudes of repentance: submission, confession, humility, and fellowship. This list is not about penance; each action is a discipline and habit that "will raise a harvest of righteousness" (James 3:18).

His readers would remember the story about Peter's adulterous betrayal of Jesus after his arrest. Peter and several fellow disciples are fishing after Jesus' death when the resurrected Jesus appears on the shore and tells them to fish on the other side of the boat. Not knowing that it is Jesus, they try the other side, and the net becomes full of fish. John says to Peter, "It is the Lord." Then Jesus invites these men to breakfast, and "when they had finished eating, Jesus said to Simon Peter, 'Simon son of John do you truly love me more than these?'" (John 21:15).

Can you imagine the guilt that Peter felt at that moment? However, Jesus did not prescribe acts of penance or punishment. Rather, Jesus restores Peter's calling by reminding Peter three times to "feed my lambs" (John 21:15), asking Peter each time to vow that he loves the Lord. The third time, Peter says, "Lord you know all things; you know that I love you," to which Jesus replies:

> "Feed my sheep. I tell you the truth when you were younger you dressed yourself and went where you wanted; but when you are old you will stretch out your hands,

and someone else will dress you and lead you where you do not want to go ... Then he said to him, 'Follow me!'" (John 21:17b–18)

Peter receives restoration through his action to draw near to Jesus, his submission to Jesus' call to ministry, and his desire to humbly follow Jesus. The rest is history.

James 4:13–17, "Now listen" #1.

So what does it mean to follow Jesus? James gives a specific example of subtle arrogance that undermines a commitment to follow Jesus. His example is about a habit we have of boasting about our plans for the future - "Now listen, you who say, 'Today or tomorrow we will go to this or that city, spend a year there, carry on business and make money.' Why, you do not even know what will happen tomorrow" (James 4:13, 4:14). Then he once again uses a question to get at the heart of what he wants to say: "What is your life?" (James 4:14). Then he answers the question:

> You are a mist that appears for a little while and then vanishes ... You ought to say, "If it is the Lord's will, we will live and do this or that." As it is, you boast and brag. All such boasting is evil. Anyone, then, who knows the good he ought to do and doesn't do it, sins. (James 4:14–17)

Jesus taught this same idea in Luke 12:16–21.

> And he told them a parable: The ground of a certain rich man produced a good crop. He thought to himself, "What shall I do?" (I have no place to store my crops).
> Then he said, "This is what I'll do. I will tear down my barns and build bigger ones, and there I will store all my grain and my goods. And I'll say to myself, 'You have plenty of good things laid up for many years. Take life easy; eat, drink and be merry.'"

> But God said to him, "You fool! This very night your life will be demanded from you. Then who will get what you have prepared for yourself?"
>
> This is how it will be with anyone who stores up things for himself but is not rich toward God.

Both excerpts begin with an essential question. James asks his readers, "What is your life?" (James 4:14), and Jesus has the rich man ask himself, "What shall I do?" (Luke 12:17). These are universal questions that every person asks in search of meaning, mission, and purpose. In both cases, James and Jesus point out the foolishness of ignoring eternal values in favor of self-lordship that chooses worldly values.

James 5:1–6, "Now listen" #2.

James begins his example about boasting about the future with the words "Now Listen, you who say ..." (James 4:13). Having just written at the end of James 4:12, "But you–who are you to judge your neighbor?" the "you" audience in verse 13 would be the same - his brother believers. However, in the next "now listen" example James addresses a new audience, "Now listen you rich people" (5:1). The "you" here are not believers but are like the rich man in Jesus' parable recorded in Luke 12. James warns them that they will "weep and wail because of the misery that is coming to [them]" (James 5:1). He describes how they take advantage of workmen and hoard their money spending it on self-indulgence, to the point of even murdering innocent men.

So having said "friendship with the world is hatred toward God" (James 4:4), James takes great pains to describe what he means. First, he accuses his brother believers of behaviors that indicate double-minded motives that produce "fights and quarrels" (James 4:2), calling them to repentance and submission. Then, he warns them to not judge one another and slander one another. Next, he highlights the subtle arrogance of boasting about plans for the future. Finally, he describes the misery in store for rich people who live solely for themselves. "You have fattened yourselves in the day of slaughter" (James 5:5).

SO WHAT?

By looking at the progression of his arguments, one can see a pathway that leads away from the high way of godly wisdom onto the downward path of worldly wisdom. One enters this pathway by allowing selfish desires and motives for pleasure to cause "fights and quarrels" (James 4:2). Then if one ignores the warning for a need for repentance and submission, this pathway will lead to judgmental slander. By usurping God's sovereign role, one continues on a pathway that leads to arrogant boasting about personal plans while ignoring the Lord's will. Becoming willing to ignore the good that ought to be done is just steps away from the full hardhearted disposition that is headed for "the day of slaughter."

Because of our sinful nature, we have all taken a stroll down the pathway of worldly wisdom. In my personal example about my friend's intervention, I chose a detour off the highway of humility, submission, and repentance. I chose selfish desires over God's lordship. My reaction to my friend who spoke the truth in love to me risked a great friendship in favor of my friendship with the world. And my friendship with the world risked my relationship with my Lord. "But [James declares, Jesus] gives more grace" (James 4:6). James is willing, like my friend, to speak the truth by pointing his fellow believers and his readers to the healing power of grace, the same grace Jesus gave to Peter. So through the Spirit's convicting grace, I am thankful that I had to recognize and admit my pride and selfishness and reconcile with my friend by asking for his forgiveness.

Do you find yourself embroiled in a conflict that has detoured your journey on the pathway of godly wisdom? I recommend the resources found at www.rw360.org. RW360.org teaches relational wisdom based on biblical truth. For example, one helpful acrostic, SOG, teaches the value of Self-awareness + Others-awareness + God-awareness when inevitable conflict disrupts peace and harmony between believers. Being self-aware is akin to looking in the mirror to discern my emotions and how they control my actions. Being other-aware is the act of genuinely considering the emotions of others and how I am affecting them. Being God-aware is bringing my findings to my Lord and asking him to work His will and purpose through me.

From RW Acrostics in Action, rw360.org:

- **S**elf-aware: How am I feeling and acting?
- **O**ther-aware: How are others feeling? How am I affecting them?
- **G**od-aware: What is God up to?

Relational wisdom, in essence, is the desire and ability to obey Jesus's timeless command, "You shall love the Lord your God with all your heart … and love your neighbor as yourself" (Matt. 22:37–39). In modern terms, "relational wisdom may be defined as your ability to discern emotions, interests, and abilities in yourself and others, to interpret this information in the light of God's Word, and to use these insights to manage your responses and relationships successfully." (RW Acrostics in Action, rw360.org)

CHAPTER 12 JAMES 4:1–5:6 STUDY GUIDE

1. **Read James 4:1–5.**
   - What is the problem?

     o Four questions about the problem
       1. "What causes fights and quarrels among you?" (James 4:1)
          a. How would you answer this question?

       2. "Don't they come from your desires that battle within you?" (James 4:1)
          a. Do you agree or disagree? Why?

       3. "Don't you know that friendship with the world is hatred toward God?" (James 4:4)
          a. Do you agree or disagree? Why?

       4. "Or do you think Scripture says without reason that the spirit he caused to live in us envies intensely?" (as a result of our fallenness James 4:5)
          a. What do you think is the idea in this question?

2. **Read James 4:6–12.**
   o State the solutions that address the problem.

   - (James 4:7)

- (James 4:8)

- (James 4:9)

- (James 4:10)

- (James 4:11, 4:12)

3. **Read James 4:13–17 and Proverbs 27:1 and 16:9.**
   - What is the issue here? Is this just about not planning for the future? How does this follow in context?

4. **Read James 5:1–6.** How does this passage sum up or reflect James 4:1–17?

5. Using our insights from James 4:1–5:6, how would you word exhortation #6?

   Exhortation #6: Post-resurrection godly wisdom …

SO WHAT?

Do you have a personal story that answers the *so what* question about what we have studied this week?

13

PRAYER CHANGES LIVES

James 5:7–20

"My brothers" exhortation #7: Post-resurrection wisdom maintains an eternal perspective by being patient, standing firm, and practicing powerful prayer.

PATIENT PRAYER

James begins his seventh instruction about living out godly wisdom with two words: "Be patient." In the following sentences, he repeats this idea. After highlighting the example of how a farmer patiently waits for the harvest, in verse 8 he writes, "Be patient and stand firm." As an example of true patience, in James 5:10, he points to the prophets who "in the face of suffering … spoke in the name of the Lord." Finally, Job is cited for his great patient endurance despite overwhelming suffering.

James knows that prayer requires patience and resolve. What is your experience with prayer? Have you ever kept a prayer journal? During an especially challenging time of my life, I kept a prayer journal because I found that writing down my prayers helped me to voice my thoughts, my doubts, my requests, my pleas, and recite my faith. Through journaling, I recognized the need for patience. In fact, over those years, I would go back to reread my prayers only to find my requests repeated almost verbatim on the exact or close to the same date each year. Infrequently, I did see that some of my requests had been answered, but not necessarily the way I had anticipated. And by answered, I mean that there was a clear event or development that addressed my request. On the other hand, I don't want to imply that God's silence meant there was no answer for most of my prayers. Often God's silence is an answer: I am to be patient, stand firm in my faith, and wait on the Lord.

James tells his brother believers they are to be patient "until the Lord's coming" (James 5:7). Just as the farmer waits for the annual autumn and spring rains, believers are to look forward to the Lord's return because it is the only event that is guaranteed to finalize all our prayer requests. Solomon wrote in his wisdom instruction, "Let love and faithfulness never leave you; bind them around your neck, write them on the tablet of your heart ... Trust in the Lord with all your heart, and lean not on our own understanding; in all your ways acknowledge him, and he will make your paths straight" (Prov. 3:3, 3:5–6). Patience is a godly discipline that requires trust and faithfulness while standing firm in a fickle world.

The enemies of patience and trust are grumbling and suffering. We speak to God, and we hear nothing back. We repeat our requests over and over. Yet we dare not grumble to God, so we become impatient and grumble about our circumstances or against our fellow believers. Then inevitable suffering in a broken creation wears us down, and instead of faithfully persevering, we become demanding, leaning on our own understanding. This erosion of faith is subtle. So James reminds us of the prophets, in general, and Job, specifically, who persevered and were blessed because "The Lord is full of compassion and mercy" (James 5:11).

I have noticed that a sure warning of an erosion of my faith occurs when I begin to jump right into my prayers with requests and demands for answers. Firstly, I think I urgently need answers in my timeline. Then my mindset shifts away from worshipful prayer that begins with seeking God. So I begin my prayer pleading with God, and then move toward demanding answers from Him. That mindset forgets that the Lord is full of compassion and mercy but instead focuses on blaming God for not giving me what I want. Like a spoiled child, I become possessed by my demands forgetting that becoming mature in my faith requires perseverance and "perseverance must finish its work so that [I] may be mature and complete, not lacking anything" (James 1:4).

Next, James returns to the theme of lack of control of our tongues in James 5:12: "Above all, my brothers, do not swear—not by heaven or by earth or by anything else." Sam Allberry, in his book *James for You*, writes,

> Once again he [James] turns our attention to the significance of how we speak ... Twice we are reminded in this short section of how, as we seek to wait patiently in the trials of this life, our tongues have the capacity to spoil everything. And once again, he attaches a solemn warning: "Above all, my brothers and sisters, do not swear – not by heaven or by earth or by anything else. All you need to say is a simple 'Yes' or 'No'. Otherwise you will be condemned" (5:12). ... James is not abruptly changing subjects here. His prohibition against swearing is a further application of the patience that he has been calling for through this section ... The swearing of oaths is another expression of the double-mindedness that has been characterizing many of his readers and undermining the credibility of their Christian confession. The particular oaths that James has in mind seem to involve invoking God's name to underline the reliability of a promise. (p. 145)

If I am patient, prayerful, and persevering there is no need to use God's name to make a promise reliable. God's name is not to be used as a guarantee or a symbol of my piousness. James is suggesting that choosing to use God's name is an attempt to pose as pious just to make a promise. In other words, the danger of using God's name to swear an oath is my attempt to use God to get what I want. As persons of faith, we are to let our "Yes" be yes, and our "No" be no (James 5:12).

Additionally, in our culture, using God's name has become anything but honoring in everyday speech. God's name is misused. Additionally, the offensively banal taking of Jesus' name is now acceptable in print media, on TV, and in movies throughout our culture. So in this passage, James's point is that our speech will reveal whom we truly worship and honor in our hearts exposing our unfaithful divided hearts when we use God's name flippantly.

James 5:13–18 answers the question: *Why* is this important? In short, James writes, "The prayer of a righteous man is powerful" (James 5:16). Prayer offered in faith overcomes trouble, heals sickness, increases happiness, and provides forgiveness. For evidence, James cites Elijah as a powerful example of patient prayer. When Ahab became king of Israel, he married Jezebel and began to serve Baal instead of the LORD, Elijah was sent by God to oppose Baal worship. For three and a half long years, Ahab sought to kill Elijah because Elijah had prayed that it would not rain to demonstrate that God was displeased with Ahab. James's audience would know the amazing story of Elijah's answered prayers recorded in 1 Kings 18. Elijah, in a prayer duel with the priests of Baal, calls down fire from heaven. When all the people saw this they "fell prostrate and cried, "The LORD–he is God! The LORD–he is God!" (1 Kings 18:39).

SO WHAT?

We serve the same LORD that Elijah served! Additionally, we have received grace and forgiveness as a result of Jesus' death and resurrection. In God's eyes we are righteous, not because of what we did but because Christ died in our place, paying the punishment we deserved. As a result, we have access to God. As God's redeemed sons and daughters, we can boldly approach our all-powerful Father to confidently offer intercession for others, knowing that prayer changes lives. Because of what Jesus did for us, we are able to patiently practice powerful prayer as impactful ambassadors for the kingdom of God. This idea leads to James's conclusive exhortation.

"My brothers" exhortation #8: Others-centered mature and complete faith always looks to turn a sinner from the error of his way. Godly wisdom saves lives! (James 5:19–20).

> My Brothers, if one of you should wander from the truth and someone should bring him back, remember this: *Whoever turns a sinner from the error of his way will save him from death and cover a multitude of sins.* (James 5: 19–20)

James's concluding summation statement is a capstone for his entire letter. He has preached in this letter that godly wisdom is not just about the edification of the believer so that the believer will stay on the high way to eternal life but, it is also about how the mission of wisdom is efficacious for those who have wandered from the truth and are lost. Looking back with a missional perspective at James's prior seven exhortations, one can discern that each instruction points to the ultimate purpose of saving lives. See the list below:

1. James 1:2–18 is a call to single-minded belief because "He [God] chose to give us birth through the word of truth, that we might be a kind of first fruits of all he created" (James 1:18). *Single-minded faith saves one from a wasteful life and leads to fruitfulness that produces more fruit.*
2. James 1:19–27 is a call to "listen to the word" and "do what it says" because by "not forgetting what he has heard but doing it—he [the believer] will be blessed in what he does, *'and, by doing what the word says, he will produce "religion that God accepts as pure and faultless" such as: "to look after orphans and widows in their distress."'*
3. James 2:1–13 is a call to not show favoritism but to show mercy instead of judgment. "Mercy triumphs over judgment" (James 2:13). *Mercy blesses others.*
4. James 2:14–3:12 is a call to verify one's faith through actions and words because "faith without deeds is dead" (James 2:26). The actions of faith heroes listed in Hebrews 11, like Abraham and Rahab who are mentioned in this passage, accomplished God's divine purpose of blessing his people. *True faith will produce*

consistent outcomes. However, James also warns that we should not "praise our Lord and Father, and ... [then] curse men who have been made in God's likeness" (James 3:9). And likewise we should not be offering "out of the same mouth praise and cursing" (James 3:10), because out of the overflow of our hearts our words betray our selfish motives and contradict our faith.

5. James 3:13–18 is a call to reject earthly wisdom that is unspiritual and of the devil but embrace godly wisdom's values—"pure ... peace-loving, considerate, submissive, full of mercy ... impartial and sincere," because *godly wisdom values "a harvest of righteousness."*
6. James 4:1–5:6 is a call to end all quarrels and fights, but rather pursue a single-minded relationship with God that changes a selfish focus into a godly focus by submitting with a humble heart the desire to draw near to God. James warns that *double-minded "self-indulgence [will lead to] fattening yourself in the day of slaughter"* (James 5:5).
7. James 5:7–18 is a call to boldly and *patiently approach our all-powerful Father to confidently offer intercession for others knowing that prayer changes lives.*

James's seven "my brothers" instructions can be summed up this way: Mature, single-minded persevering faith influences others for the eternal kingdom of God. In general, James maintains that each believer has been placed in a position of influence for God's purposes. As followers of Jesus, James maintains we are called to be missional within our spheres of influence. In marriage, family, friendships, and work relationships, we have opportunities to be others-centered and ministry aware. In his short but hard-hitting letter to believers, James has insisted that our faith, mindset, attitudes, words, behaviors, and deeds, must be aligned with the "word of truth [so] that we might be a kind of first fruits" (James1:18) that will produce a "harvest of righteousness" (James 3:18) in the spheres of influence we have been given.

Jesus, in his Sermon on the Mount, powerfully illustrated the foundational truths for James's exhortations.

> You are the salt of the earth. But if the salt loses its saltiness, how can it be made salty again? It is no longer good for anything except to be thrown out and be trampled by men. You are the light of the world. A city on a hill cannot be hidden. Neither do people light a lamp and put it under a bowl. Instead they put it on a stand, and it gives light to everyone in the house. In the same way let your light shine before men, that they may see your good deeds and praise the Father in heaven. (Matt. 5:13–16)

Jesus' words motivate me to ask two important questions about my faith and actions. Where in my faith walk am I losing my saltiness? Do my deeds, attitudes, words, and intentions influence those in my spheres of influence to glorify my Father in heaven? Jesus' brother James's letter to believers describes earmarks of what it takes to be "the salt of the earth" and "the light of the world" (Matt. 5:13–16).

According to James, this is what salt and light looks like:

- Single-minded faith
- Listening to and acting on God's word
- Serving others by extending mercy instead of judgment
- Faithful deeds
- Embracing eternal values
- Humble submission to God
- Powerful prayer
- Rescuing lost lives

But James is also bold enough to confront me with what it looks like to lose my saltiness and dim my light. According to James, lost saltiness and darkness look like this:

- Double-minded doubt
- Impatient demands and anger
- Immoral thoughts and evil actions
- Quarreling and fighting to get one's way
- Mouthing faith without acting faith

- Praising God but also cursing men
- Double-minded prayers
- Putting self before others

SO WHAT?

Quite simply, James illustrates what it looks like to save or lose one's life. Godly wisdom is about a single-minded preoccupation with eternal values. Worldly wisdom is about double-minded living for the moment and for self. The first is pure and purposeful. The second is about seeking personal advantage. The first produces changed lives. The second produces conflict and "is earthly, unspiritual, of the devil" (James 3:15). The first produces "a harvest of righteousness" (James 3:18). The second produces "disorder and every evil practice" (James 3:16).

He concludes his letter with a powerful statement: "Remember this: Whoever turns a sinner from the error of his way will save him from death and cover a multitude of sins" (James 5:20).

CHAPTER 13 JAMES 5:7–20 STUDY GUIDE

1. **Look back to chapter 12 study guide.**
   a. How did you word exhortation #6?

2. **Review James 5:7–18, "My brothers" instruction #7.**
   What are the behaviors of being patient?
   - (James 5:8–11)
     - (James 5:8) [Do]
       - Why?
     - (James 5:99) "Don't
       - Why?
     - (James 5:10–11) Example
       - Why?
   - (James 5:12)
     - "Do not"
       - Why?
   - (James 5:13–18)
     - The practice of patient …

- Example

3. **Read James 5:19–20, "My brothers" instruction #8.**
   - Why is this the final instruction?

     - What? (James 5:19)

     - Why? (James 5:20)

Summary of 8 Post-Resurrection "My Brothers" Instructions

1. *Mature and complete faith* grows out of the soil of single-minded joyful perseverance. (James 1:2–18)
2. *Humbly rid yourself* of all anger, moral filth, and evil so that you can live out Jesus's words by serving others. (James 1:19–27)
3. *True love* always speaks and acts with mercy and without judgment or favoritism. (James 2:1–13)
4. *True faith* will always be evidenced by its deeds. (James 2:14–25)
5. *Pay attention to your words.* Your tongue will reveal your *true values and beliefs.* Godly wisdom values: Be pure, peace-loving, considerate, submissive, merciful, impartial, and sincere. (James 3:1–12)
6. *Humbly submit to God* by extending mercy and peace to others and by rejecting envy and selfish ambition.(James 3:13–18, also 4:1–5:1–6)
7. *Maintain your eternal perspective* in midst of inevitable suffering by being patient, standing firm, and practicing powerful prayer and praise. Prayer changes lives. (James 5:7–18)
8. *Mature and others-centered faith* always looks to turn a sinner from the error of his way. (James 5:19–20)

14

SO WHAT?

In a post-resurrection world, godly wisdom must be single-minded because faith-infused, single-minded, godly wisdom changes lives.

In his letter, James earnestly admonishes, exhorts, and instructs believers about the power of single-minded and effective faith. His message to first-century Christians is even more trenchant for twenty-first-century believers living in a postmodern culture that turns capital-*T* Truth into lowercase-*t* truth, making truth malleable to fit any situation involving ego, ambition, and autonomy. In fact, twenty-first-century people are multi-minded, not just double-minded, because we are influenced by many voices declaring self-serving lowercase truths. Because worldly wisdom celebrates diversity in opinions and tolerance of many points of view, individual autonomy is worshipped instead of godly authority. James' instructions about God's authority for first-century believers—to be eternally focused and single-mindedly missional—is even more relevant for twenty-first-century believers. His warnings that all believers must examine their mindset, actions, deeds, prayers, and words echo Paul's words in 1 Corinthians 9:22, where he declares that he has "become all things to all men so that by all possible means [he] might save some."

Hundreds of years before John and James, Solomon taught that "the fear of the LORD is the beginning of wisdom, and knowledge of the Holy One is understanding" (Prov. 9:10). In other words, eternally focused wisdom is fearfully aware that godly wisdom begins with knowledge of the Holy

One resulting in reverence for the Almighty Creator. In God's timing, John introduced Jesus as the Holy One, declaring that Jesus is the way, the *Truth,* and the life (John 14:6). By describing Jesus as the embodiment of godly wisdom, John, in his well-known chapter 3 about Nicodemus and John the Baptist, describes how to become a believer by seeking *Truth,* testing *Truth,* believing *Truth,* and acting on that *Truth.* Then in God's timing, after Jesus' death and resurrected appearance witnessed by his brother and many others, James instructs believers about authentic true faith that rescues lives in our post-resurrection world.

As two compelling voices from the advent of Christianity, John and James are still relevant over two thousand years later calling on believers to grow in their knowledge and understanding of the Holy One. This all-important message bridges Solomon's message that the pathway of godly wisdom leads to life. John's Gospel introduces the Holy One who taught about how belief leads to eternal life and godly wisdom is gospel wisdom—the good news that rescues us from the downward pathway of destructive worldly wisdom. After Jesus' resurrection, James challenges believers with clear and practical exhortations about how believers are to conduct themselves in a fallen world that "wanders [away] from truth" (James 5:19).

Our three key questions—What? Why? And so what?—provide a lens for our study of post-resurrection godly wisdom.

The following are questions and succinct summary answers for the *what* and *why* of mature godly wisdom:
What? Godly wisdom promotes flourishing. Worldly wisdom leads to destruction.
Why? Jesus, the embodiment of godly wisdom, modeled and taught what believing faith leads away from the road to destruction and to the highway to life eternal.

The *what* and *why* instructions about godly wisdom set up the anchoring question: *So what* difference does godly wisdom make?

1. While growth in knowledge and understanding of the Holy One is not an end in itself, it is the beginning of living wisely with eternity in view. When we live humbly with a faith-infused single-minded purpose by maintaining an eternal perspective, we influence others to join us on the highway to the everlasting kingdom of God.
2. Solomon's wisdom curriculum in Proverbs 1–9 taught that worldly wisdom is a fast track to destruction. His theme is that godly wisdom begins with the fear of the LORD and the knowledge of the Holy One. The *so what* of his teaching declared that godly wisdom leads to a rewarding long life (Prov. 9:10–12). However, he acknowledges that this is the beginning of understanding wisdom. In Solomon's world, a beginning will always eventually lead to an ending—death. Four hundred years later, John's Gospel declares a new beginning—the Word who was with God and was God (John 1:1). He came to shine a light on the pathway to becoming children of God. He came to be "the way and truth and the life" (John 14:6) as the embodiment of godly wisdom. The gospel message that "Jesus is the Christ, the Son of God, and that by believing you may have life [eternal] in His name" (John 20:31) answers the *so what* question about how precious godly wisdom truly is.
3. However, godly wisdom is not just about a way to live wisely. That is why, in his letter, James exhorts believers to apply wisdom to their daily living in a fallen world, so that sinners will be turned from the error of their ways and will be saved from eternal death. Godly wisdom is gospel wisdom, and gospel wisdom is the difference between life and death. Jesus Christ took on our sins and died a death we deserved so that we can live wisely with eternity in view.

One last way to look at God's inspired words about godly wisdom through Solomon, John, and James: Solomon's instruction reveals the *what*s of knowledge of godly wisdom by providing seventeen "my Son" precepts. John's Gospel provides the *why* of godly wisdom in Jesus' message about believing Truth as the way to becoming a child of God. Finally, James's letter describes eight "My brothers" exhortations challenging believers to live out the *so what* behaviors of daily living wisely with eternity in view.

"Knowledge" and "understanding" of the "Holy One" is "the beginning of wisdom" (Prov. 9:10) "but fools despise wisdom and discipline" (Prov. 1:7). How, then, will you apply "so what" wisdom single-minded faith "in humility that comes from wisdom?" (James 3:13).

CPSIA information can be obtained
at www.ICGtesting.com
Printed in the USA
BVHW040250140922
646955BV00001B/49